Issues and Responses

VOLUME ONE

A collection of Articles, Speeches
and Commentaries
by Trade Unionist Dennis de Peiza,
on Industrial Relations, Education, Cultural,
Socio-Economic and Political Issues

DENNIS ST. C. DE PEIZA
M.A., B.A. (Hons.) Cert. Ed.

Copyright © 2006

Regional Management Services Inc.
P.O. Box 845, Bridgetown, Barbados
www.regionalmanagementservices.com
Email: rmsinc@sunbeach.net

All rights reserved. No part of this publication may be produced or transmitted in any form or by any means, electronic or mechanical, including photocopying, recording, or any information storage and retrieval system, without the permission of the author.

de Peiza, Dennis: Issues and Responses, Volume One
December, 2013

ISBN 978-149-4361-96-9 (paperback)

This publication contains both published and unpublished articles. In addition it includes speeches made and papers presented at various fora; the contents of some of which were carried in part in the print and electronic media.

Cover Design & Layout: Editions Publishing
                                editionspublishing@gmail.com

Author's Profile

Dennis de Peiza is a Barbadian trade unionist of more than 25 years' experience. He has served in the offices of President, General Secretary and Public Relations Officer of the Barbados Union of Teachers, 3rd Vice President and trustee of the Caribbean Union of Teachers, and is the current General Secretary of the Congress of Trade Unions and Staff Association of Barbados.

He is a qualified and trained teacher who has served 33 years in the teaching profession. Apart from spending most of his teaching career at the secondary school level, he also taught at the Barbados Community College in Barbados as an assistant tutor in History.

His professional qualifications include the Erdiston Teacher's Training Certificate, awarded by the Erdiston Teachers' College (Barbados), and the certificate in Education Management and Administration, attained from the University of the West Indies, Cave Hill Campus.

His academic profile reflects that he holds a Bachelor of Arts (BA) Hons. Degree in History and Sociology from the University of the

West Indies, and a Masters Degree (MA) in Public Administration, from the University of Baltimore, Maryland, USA.

As a practising trade unionist he has been exposed to formal training, and has successfully completed courses of studies at The Trade Union Education Institute, Mona Campus, University of the West Indies, and at the National Labour College, Maryland, USA.

He is known for his many articles and commentaries on Labour Relations and Education issues that have been published in the Barbados Union of Teachers' magazine, OUTLOOK, the Barbados Workers' Union publication, THE UNIONIST and the Caribbean Union of Teachers' magazine, CARICULTURE. In addition he has written several articles that have been published under the guest columns of the NATION and the BARBADOS ADVOCATE newspapers.

This publication serves to capture the many views expressed by the author on the topical labour socio-economic, political and educational issues in Barbados during the last decade of the 1990's and the first decade of the 21st Century.

Author's Note

Over the years, I have written extensively on industrial relations issues. In sharing my views with the public at large, I have used the medium of the print media to inform and educate.

I am pleased to offer you my first publication. Its contents are primarily articles and commentaries that have been published over the years, as well as speeches made at several fora.

It is my hope that you find this publication interesting reading, and one that you deem worthy to recommend to your many associates, colleagues and friends.

It is envisaged that this publication will prove to be an excellent resource for those undertaking research. I strongly recommend this book as a source of reading for students at the tertiary level, students of Industrial Relations and Human Resources Management, trade unionists from the level of leadership to that of shop stewards, and trainers within the labour movement.

It is anticipated that this publication will make interesting reading for those persons who find pleasure in reviewing contemporary issues and developments that characterize a given society.

The contents will prove to be insightful in broadening your knowledge and understanding of the issues and challenges to be faced in the practice of industrial relations. More over, it is expected that you will have a greater sense of appreciation for best practices to be engaged in the pursuit of creating an ideal industrial relations climate.

I take this opportunity to thank all persons who have contributed in making this publication possible.

DENNIS DE PEIZA, M.A., B.A. (Hons) Cert. Ed.

Table of Contents

Chapter 1
LABOUR AND SOCIAL DEVELOPMENT 1

The Right to Decent Work 1
Review of the Workings of the Social Partnership 6
Technological Change and the Credit
Union Movement. 15
National Employment and Migrant
Guyanese Labour. 19
The Free Movement of Caribbean Labour. 23
Identifying the Labour Movement's Agenda for 2004 27
Wages and Salaries Negotiations 31
Developing a Workplace Crisis lan. 35
Industrial Harmony. 38
Worker Recognition. 42

Chapter 2
**TRADE UNIONISM - ITS GROWTH
AND DEVELOPMENT** 45

Trade Unionism - A Sense of Power 45
An Overview of CTUSAB - Its Formation,
Role and Achievements. 48
Teacher Unions and Challenges in Education. 58
B.U.T Flaunts Proud Record 71
Concerns About Failing System 75
Workers' Rights Under Attack 79

Chapter 3
PROBLEMS IN EDUCATION 82

World Congress on Teaching 82
Societal Values Falling by the Wayside. 89
Dress Codes Ignored 94
Addressing Declining Values Amongst Our Youth 98
Violence in Schools: What Can Be Done
To Protect Teachers? 104
Remarks to ILO Workshop 108
Tribute to John Henry Cumberbatch 111
Lengthening the School Year 118
Sports Versus Academics. 123

Chapter 4
HEALTH 126

The Health Status of the Workforce. 126
Occupational Safety and Health. 129
Prevention of Alcoholism and Drug Dependency 134

Chapter 5
RIGHTS AND RESPONSIBILITIES 137

Each Individual Should be Responsible
for His/Her Actions 137
Absenteeism in the Public Service 148
Homosexuality and Teachers: Protection
of the Rights of Gays and Lesbians. 151

Chapter 6
GENERAL PRESENTATIONS **154**

Challenge to Teachers - Observing the
Professional Code of Ethics. 154
Teaching: A Profession in Transition 158
Gender Relations - Its Implications for Teaching 162
Promoting Improved Labour Management Relations . . . 164
Globalisation: A Challenge to Remain Competitive 168
Challenge to Workers And Management. 171
Fraternal Greetings to BWU's
62nd Annual Delegates' Conference (2003) 175
Honour for Sir Roy. 178
ILO/CIDA Regional Child Labour Project. 185
Delivering High Quality Service. 189
No Need for Complacency 192
CSME and the Implications For
Immigration Control 195
Social Development Policy Challenge of Barbados. 203
The Employee Work Ethic. 210

ABBREVIATIONS. **215**

Chapter One

Labour and Social Development

The Right to Decent Work

The growing number of complaints made by workers about perceived exploitation at the hands of their employers, begs the question as to whether the right to 'decent work is being undermined by some unscrupulous employers in this country. To the average Barbadian employer, the notion of decent work may be linked to the matter of pay. It must be stressed that decent work relates to more than pay. Arguably, it should extend to the feeling of ownership by all employees.

According to the Glossary of 'Industrial Relations and Related Terms and Concepts For Trade Unions', as produced by the International Labour Organization (ILO Caribbean Office) decent work "Implies access to employment in conditions of freedom; the recognition of basic rights at work, guaranteeing the absence of discrimination or harassment; an income enabling one to satisfy basic economic, social and family needs and responsibilities; an adequate level of social protection for the worker and family members; and the right to participation and a voice at work, directly or indirectly through self-chosen representative organizations."

Barbados' acceptance of the ILO's concept of decent work is reflected in Section 4.2 of Protocol 4. However, what stands out as a significant factor is reflected in Section 4.3 (d) of Protocol 4, which reads: "The Social Partners also agree that such a national employment policy should specifically: Ensure the provision of those conditions which accord with an understanding of the right to decent work, including a written statement of the particulars of employment, the payment of adequate wages and salaries, reasonable working times, satisfactory arrangements for wholesome conditions at work, for security when ill or otherwise reasonably absent from work, and for the application of suitable and acceptable benefits on retirement".

Substantiated reports have confirmed that some local employers are guilty of not observing the notion of decent work. Some have been known to have made arbitrary changes to the conditions of employment. One example to be cited, relates to the dismissal of an employee by a business in the north of the island for failure to come to work on Saturdays. Under the contract of employment, the employee was required to complete a forty-hour work week, Monday through Friday, work on Saturday having been determined as being optional.

In another instance, the actions of the employer seemed aimed at penalizing the employee who fell ill on the job. In this instance, the employer sought to withhold part of a day's pay of the employee who took ill on the job, after having to be taken away to seek medical attention. The excuse tendered by the employer for withholding pay was that the employee did not sign out before leaving the compound.

In many instances weekly paid employees are the victims of dismissal, where no notice of intended termination, nor reasons for dismissal are given. In as much as these employers are not obligated under law to account for their actions, any recourse through the

Labour Department is negated by the fact that it is powerless to act.

Trade unions have at times been rendered powerless to act, as in some instances the employee involved is non-unionized, while in others, the employers have sought to immobilize the workers' representative, by laying off unionized employees, or by employing the now common trend of replacing the Barbadian Labour by immigrant contract labour.

There are reported instances where employees are forced to work in an unsafe and hazardous environment, often without safety equipment. It is said that where they refused to work in the existing conditions, they are sent home for the day, resulting in the loss of a part of the day's pay. Is this what we are to expect and accept in the work place in the 21st Century in Barbados?

Employers who pursue a path that seemingly compromises the expectations of employees in their right to decent work, ought not be allowed to continue to perpetrate such repressive behaviour in a highly developed Barbados Society, that prides itself on promoting best practices in labour management relations. If a turn around in this is to be imminent, then CTUSAB considers that greater emphasis has to be placed by the Social Partners on protection for workers who exercise their constitutional right to freedom of association.

Added to this, the Social Partners must demonstrate the commitment to this, by moving to the implementation stage, in initiating a policy that is aimed at protecting employees from arbitrary dismissal. It is simply not enough for the Social Partners to have a written policy statement that speaks explicitly to all employees being able to enjoy the right not to be unfairly dismissed, to be unfairly prevented from continued employment, to the procedure for termination of employment shall accord with the principle of natural justice, and the principles enunciated by the International Labour Organization.

If these measures were put in place to ensure compliance with these ideals, this would undoubtedly send a clear signal that every effort is being made to satisfy the requirement of one of the most important principles associated with decent work. If the intentions of the National Employment Policy as reflected in Protocol 4, are to be taken seriously, then, it is absolutely necessary that Government moves to address the many unscrupulous employment practices by enacting the Employment Rights Bill.

It is important that the matter of the Employment Rights Bill is not allowed to be placed on the back burner, for to do so would be to suggest that only lip service is to be paid to the provisions of the National Employment Policy, as set out under Protocol 4.

ILO Decent Work Caribbean Tripartite Workshop
Trinidad, March 2nd - 5th, 2004

Employers are to be cautioned that they are not free to set any terms they wish as conditions of employment. They ought to observe the fact that they have a moral obligation to their employees, not to arbitrarily impose terms and conditions of service without completing the process of dialogue with the representative body for the employees, where specific terms and conditions are not outlined in the contract of employment or by government's' regulations.

Published: Daily Nation (Newspaper) December 17th, 2003, Page 24A. Headlined: Work Standards In Doubt

Review of the Workings of the Social Partnership in Barbados

The views identified in this review on the workings of the Social Partnership as expressed by Joseph Goddard (General Secretary, NUPW), Dr. Ashwell Thomas (President, BEC), John Pilgrim (Executive Director, BARNAPCO), Ronald Jones (Member of Parliament, Opposition-DLP), and Peter Wickham, Political Scientist, UWI, Cave Hill Campus, were captured on the Voice of Barbados 92.9 FM Radio Programme: Point At Issue, aired on Sunday, June 20th, 2004.

Joseph Goddard, General Secretary of the NUPW, lamented the fact that there was a lack of equity, non-adherence to the dispute resolution procedure and the absence of an appeal mechanism relating to the resolution of grievances that involved Government as the employer of public workers, which in essence did not contribute to a meaningful social partnership

He argued that the Social Partnership was failing inasmuch that Government was paying lip service to human resources, despite the fact that it recognized this as the island's most precious assets.

In putting his view into perspective, he commented that, "when the representatives of those same resources approach Government as a partner and try to get some progress on these matters, no help is forthcoming."

Dr. Ashwell Thomas of the Barbados Employers' Confederation shared the view that an assessment of the working of the Social Partnership would not be complete if reference was not made to the subject of Prices and Incomes; which he identified as one of the main reasons associated with the development of the Social Partnership.

He opined, "to a large extent I think that it has stabilized the economy, resulting in the relative inflation of 1.58% in December of 2003 and 1.65% in February of 2004. In this regard one has to give credit to the efforts of the Social Partnership. On the question of labour management relationships, the Social Partnership as a concept needs to be widened and deepened within our society, more so at the workplace.

The Social Partnership does not prevent any of the partners from exercising independence. Each partner is obligated to act rationally and responsibly towards the resolution of disputes.

I do not believe that in real terms work place relations are any better in 2004 than they were in 1992, and for that reason I would say that in that regard the Social Partnership needs to be improved.

I make note of the whole question of 'wild cat strikes' which have been taking place, resulting in a number of man days lost to productivity. According to the Productivity Council's Report in 2003, we see where productivity is declining in Barbados. On that basis, I would say that there is need for improvement where the Social Partnership is concerned. On the question of labour and social legislation the Social Partnership seems in my mind, to be a hindrance to the creation of labour and social legislation . . .

CTUSAB 4th Biennial Conference, September 2004
From left: Canon Frank Marshall, Patrick Frost, General Secretary CTUSAB,
Sir Roy Trotman, President, Dennis de Peiza, Assistant General Secretary,
(partly hidden)

Since 1992, only one piece of legislation has been enacted, although there were several new bills, including those to amend existing legislations, introduced in that period. It would seem that once a certain partner registers objection, the initiator of the Bill retreats, rather than working through the differences with the objector.

If the Partners are unable to resolve their differences and move forward, then the partnership in my opinion is ineffective."

Ronald Jones, M.P, member of the Opposition Democratic Labour Party was himself a former President of the Barbados Union of Teachers, and one of the leaders who was a signatory to Prices and Incomes Protocol of 1991, did not consider that the Social Partnership was serving the purpose for which it was intended. According to him "The Social Partnership at this stage is a disaster." He contended that after some early success, the workers have been marginalized, by what he termed "as unequal participation".

He referred to the rigidities that management and government had adopted to the resolution of issues that affected workers in Barbados. He argued that if the Social Partnership was in fact working, there would be no need for workers to be engaged in forms of protest action. He advanced the view that if a resolution mechanism was in place to meet the legitimate needs and demands of the workers, such a process would negate the need for apparent fractures between labour, management and government.

There is a body of opinion that the shortcomings associated with the working of the Social Partnership, do not provide adequate grounds to support any claims that the Social Partnership has not worked.

It is felt that without the Social Partnership, the prevailing economic and industrial climate in the country would have been totally transformed. This claim could only be justified provided that it is reviewed against the objectives of the Social Partnership.

Using this as a guide in assessing the workings of the Social Partnership, John Pilgrim, Executive Director of the Barbados National Productivity Council (BARNAPCO) referred to the fact that one of the major objectives of the Social Partnership back in 1991 was that of maintaining the parity of the Barbados Dollar. That objective has moved through Protocols II, III and IV. In as much that the parity has been maintained, the Social Partnership has continued to work in that vein.

He commented that, "In reviewing the objective of the expansion of the economy to satisfy the need to improve competitiveness to provide the right of access to unemployment, to reduce the threat of social dislocation, caused by an unacceptably high level of employment, the fact is, when one looks at 1992 and 1993, the unemployment rate was about 25.4%. Overtime the Social Partnership has been able to work towards ensuring that this unacceptable high level of unemployment has been pushed downward, as it stands right now, to about 11.2%."

Against the background of the supporting data, he concluded that the Social Partnership has worked in realizing the objective of reducing unemployment.

The Social Partnership is also to be credited for its work in maintaining the living standards that obtained in the country. In voicing support for this, John Pilgrim contended that, "when you look at the rate of increase in the public sector, and match it against the rate of inflation, it can be said that the Social Partnership has worked to ensure that the rate increase does not run ahead of productivity increases in the country, or productivity increases on national growth."

Relative to the prevailing social climate in Barbados, the work of the Social Partnership is not to be ignored as a factor in minimizing the level of industrial unrest that has been recorded since 1991. This point of view was supported by John Pilgrim, who in comparing the number of man days lost to strikes and other forms of industrial action prior to 1993 as opposed to post 1994, concluded that there has been a considerable drop in the number of days lost. In rating how the Social Partnership has been able to deal with issues towards minimizing the number of man-days lost, he suggested that on a scale of 1-10, the partnership could be credited with an achievement rating of 7.5%.

Where on the one hand statistical evidence has been used to suggest that the incidence of loss of productive man-hours to industrial action is minimal, there is the contrary position emerging from the number of 'wild cat strikes' that have plagued the country. This widely used form of protest action, seemingly holds implications for the working of the Social Partnership. What has become evident is the fact that strained workplace relationships remain in existence.

Not withstanding the statistical evidence of limited man-days lost to industrial protest action, Pilgrim concedes that based on the spate of industrial action that has become a feature of the industrial relations landscape, it would appear that the Social Partnership had failed in meeting its objective in promoting industrial harmony.

Dr. Ashwell Thomas' observation that the overwhelming number of strikes in Barbados are due to workplace relationships arising from poor relationships between management and labour, supports Pilgrim's view regarding the partnership's failure to successfully promote industrial harmony. He expressed the opinion that this resulted because the trust and confidence level was not good. The burning question that remains is... what has contributed to the disconnect that has given rise to poor workplace relationships that in turn constrain efforts at maintaining industrial harmony? It would seem that the poor level of communication (collaboration and consultation) between management and labour, has been a single contributing factor.

Despite the failings identified with the workings of the Social Partnership, some positives have been recorded. One such achievement is manifested in the development of the incentive scheme programme within the private sector. According to John Pilgrim, statistical information available to the Barbados National

Productivity Council suggested that prior to 1993, the number of companies that had incentive schemes in place was fairly marginal. In making a comparison one decade later, the evidence available reflects that most companies have, or are developing schemes. In crediting the Social Partnership for the gains made in this respect, reference was made to the acknowledgement on the part of the Social Partners of the need to provide productivity pay to employees against the backdrop of wage freezes and marginal wages and salaries increases.

Having identified some of the failings of the Social Partnership, there remains a fundamental question to be answered. What is to be done to improve on the effectiveness in the working of the Social Partnership? In addressing this, Dr. Ashwell Thomas, President of the BEC, advanced the view that, the Partners need to show stronger commitment to the process and the overall results, rather than being occupied with the attainment of sectorial interests, even when it is evident that the national interest is likely to be compromised. Secondly, there is the need for greater involvement of leaders on the ground, through the establishment of social compacts between management and labour of individual organizations, as adjunct to the collective labour agreement where applicable. This should be based on the general principles of the Protocol. Thirdly, a massive education programme has to be developed to inform all Barbadians of the intent and purposes of the social compact and the processes involved. Fourthly, organizations are to include the principles of protocols into their employee orientation programmes; have on-going debate at different levels on what the Social Partnership means to the ordinary worker and better governance to the organizations, and the country. Finally, establish a Social Partnership Secretariat, to follow up on issues and decisions attained at the Social Partnership meetings. The terms of reference should be clearly defined, so as not to duplicate or create confusion with existing labour relations machinery."

The perceived failings in the working of the Social Partnership have given rise in some quarters to the idea of withdrawal from the partnership. This notion of withdrawal was an option cited by the National Union of Public Workers. According to its General Secretary, Joseph Goddard, the advantages of being in the Social Partnership are miniscule as far as the NUPW is concerned.

It is a seemingly fair comment that considering that the International Labour Organization has hailed the development of the Social Partnership model in Barbados as a 'model of best practice', any notion of withdrawing by any one Partner or organizations within any of the groupings, would tend to reflect a level of immaturity. Moreover, such an action may be deemed as premature, considering the changing nature of industrial relations practice, which is now centred on the process of dialogue.

Opposition Member of Parliament, Ronald Jones, made an appropriate response to the suggestion of withdrawal from the Partnership by citing that the process should not be abandoned, considering that the current times are going to be even more difficult as far as industrial relations practices are concerned. He stressed the need to ensure that unions remained equal partners in the process and demanded the fullest respect they deserve by any means necessary, from the other members of the Social Partners.

Following on the analysis presented, a picture has emerged that there is a need to address improvements in the workings of the Social Partnership. Evidently, there is a need for a greater level of collaboration and consultation to take place beyond the leadership of the Social Partners. It requires a commitment and understanding to collaboration and consultation that had seemingly not transcended to the lower and middle echelons of management, or the lower and middle echelons of leadership between management and labour.

Towards advancing the cause of the Social Partnership, it is felt that the partners need to rid themselves of their concerns over jurisdictional issues. Where jurisdictional issues surfaced in the past, and have remained unresolved, such have served to undermine the unity amongst the Social Partners or within the ranks of an individual grouping. Moreover, this state of affairs can be described as a contributing factor that leads to the compromising of the integrity and stability of the Social Partnership.

It would seem that there is the acceptance that the concepts and principles for which the Social Partnership stands, are good. Notwithstanding the shortcomings identified in the workings of the Social Partnership in Barbados, it remains the preferred approach to be followed in meeting the challenges of industrial relations in the globalized environment of the 21st Century.

Hence, there is merit in the assertion of Barbadian Political Scientist, Peter Wickham that the fact that the Social Partnership has withstood the test of time, is enough to satisfy all interests that the Social Partnership is the 21st Century approach to trade unionism, and to dealing with problems.

Technological Change and the Credit Union Movement

From time immemorial, reforms have been known to characterize the global society, with emerging changes having impacted significantly on the way we do things. In accepting the view that change is inevitable, it boils down to an acceptance of a transformation in the process of the way we do things.

In retrospect, one recalls the Industrial Revolution of the 18th century and the impact that it had in transforming the world. Indeed the technological advancements of that era drastically changed the world at all levels.

In today's world, rapid technological changes have continued to unfold, leading to the increasing automation of the business world. Accompanying this is a wave of new knowledge, skills, approaches and methodologies, and indeed, a distinct change in our social life.

With "reform" being the buzz word which has taken the Barbadian society by storm, the local credit union movement will, like many other areas of Barbadian life, be expected to re-examine itself with a view of improving on the way it conducts its business. As a major arm of the Barbadian financial sector, such reform is inevitable.

Anticipating the response of the credit union movement to the challenges of the 21st century, gives cause for serious consideration of the redirection which ought to characterize it in this new age.

Already we have witnessed the first step taken by one of the major credit unions on the island, the Public Workers' Credit Union, in introducing the ATM system. This may be considered a progressive move, as it provides a more efficient service to members, while at the same time, allowing them 24-hour access to their savings.

This development is indeed laudable, but it is highly questionable as to how extensively such could be reflected across the spectrum of the local movement.

For such an elaborate investment to be worthwhile, it would require that credit unions which seek to put this technology in place, should account for a large enough membership, that would utilize this facility on a regular basis.

In the context of the Barbadian setting, few credit unions could justify investing such large sums of money, considering their limited membership and the scope in attracting the members. Outside of the Public Workers' Credit Union, the City of Bridgetown and possibly the Barbados Workers' Union credit unions, there are few other credit unions on the island that could justifiably contemplate introducing the ATM as a new service to their membership.

There can be little doubt that this new technology, which has been introduced by the traditional banking sector, will place some pressure on the local credit union movement, as it seeks to compete in attempting to meet the needs of credit unionists.

Herein lies the challenge to the credit union movement to ensure that it is a part of the reform thrust and not left behind in the fast changing environment. This would necessitate either the amalgamation of a number of the smaller credit unions, or the implementation of a system which could allow members of various credit unions to access funds and conduct other forms of business through a shared ATM system, which has a programme specifically designed to accommodate such.

With the heavy emphasis on the informatics and computerization, local credit unions could hardly exist in the current environment if they failed to incorporate computerization as part of their operations. But what does this mean for the smaller local credit unions, in particular, those whose financial base could serve as a limitation in keeping pace with such development?

This means that there must be a process of consolidation within the movement. No other grouping than the Barbados Co-operative Credit Union League is appropriately placed to develop a system, which can be accessed by all credit unions that are desirous of using the facility. Such an initiative would require major funding but this is indeed what is to be expected of a parent body that is committed to the development of the movement on the whole, and the efficiency of the operations of its member units.

This reform process goes beyond technological improvement but also addresses the question of improved management within the movement. In an attempt to attain this, it would be necessary for the individual credit unions to re-assess the performances of their management personnel. More so, their suitability for the task(s) before hand must be considered. The question of suitability relates to the individual's present skills, which must be assessed in order to identify whether training or retraining is required to either sharpen or improve on individual management skills.

In relation to this, modern day credit unions need to equip

themselves with persons who are trained managers, and not with management personnel whose only experience is limited to hands-on experience in the operations of a credit union. The local credit union movement in Barbados has long outgrown this type of thinking. It is imperative that those associated with the movement recognize that it represents a major part of the island's financial sector.

We must become increasingly aware, that as part of the progressive business world, every local credit union must seek to have full time staff. They must employ persons who possess the expertise and who are available during the course of a working day to respond immediately to the needs and/or concerns of the people they serve.

The effectiveness and the efficiency of the local credit union movement will be a matter of scrutiny of the business world and indeed all credit unionists. Should the movement fail to respond appropriately to the challenges of this era of reform, its stagnation would obviously become evident, and its efficiency and viability would become highly questionable.

Published: Co-op Vision Magazine January 29th, 1996

The National Employment Policy and the Issue of Migrant Guyanese Labour

The ongoing debate on the subject of Guyanese migrant labour could be better served if attention was directed to the issues of the management of migrant labour into Barbados, and the treatment and exploitation being experienced by migrants. In addition, focus should also be placed on addressing the implications that large scale migrant labour holds for continual employment of Barbadian labour.

There is no denying that the policy of the free movement of labour in the region is one that is supported by the Barbados labour movement. It is however, important to recognize that this can only be meaningfully achieved in a diverse Caribbean society, provided that systems that lend to the safeguarding of the rights and entitlements of employees are developed. As it currently stands the lack of uniformity in the application of labour standards and legislation across the region, allows for some compromising to take place. This accounts for the actions attributed to some unscrupulous employers.

The current Barbadian experience suggests that there is evidence of exploitation of Guyanese labour. Some employers in the construction industry have been guilty of engaging in some unacceptable practices where Guyanese workers are afforded terms and conditions of services that are less favourable than those offered to Barbadians.

The immediate fall out associated with the recruitment of Guyanese labour is that employers in the construction sector are moving to lay off Barbadian artisans, and replace them by Guyanese labour at lower rates of pay. It would appear that Guyanese labour can be imported overnight. The accessibility and availability of cheaper Guyanese labour therefore places the employment of the Barbadian artisans in particular, under threat.

Considering the provisions of Protocol IV as it relates to the National Employment Policy, CTUSAB would be failing in its obligation to the people of Barbados, if it did not speak out against the many indifferent practices that have emerged. It therefore becomes necessary to remind all and sundry of Section 4.3 of Protocol IV which reads:

"The Social Partners also agree that such a national employment policy should...

d) Ensure the provision of these conditions which accord with an understanding of the right to decent work, including a written statement of particulars of employment, the payment of adequate wages and salaries, reasonable working times, satisfactory arrangements for wholesome conditions at work, for security when ill or otherwise absent from work and for the application of suitable and acceptable benefits on retirement."

(e) Seek to protect existing employment and to provide jobs to all Barbadians who are available for and desirous of work, to make such work as productive as possible, and to ensure the freedom of choice of employment in an environment void of any form of discrimination where workers have the greatest possible opportunity to qualify for, and to use their skills and potential in

Workers on Construction Site

a job well suited to them."

The Congress has to remain vigilant in its efforts to safeguard the interest of Barbadian labour. The exploitation of Caribbean labour cannot be condoned in any form. CTUSAB is committed to promoting the concept of "Decent Work" and hence denounces the actions on the part of any employer or agent of the employer in attempting to deny Caribbean nationals their rights as workers, or seeks to exploit them as the employer sees fit.

Barbadians should not allow themselves to be swayed by the emotions of the issue, but instead focus on what is acceptable in the hiring and treatment of all labour. Further, Barbadians should not be myopic in their outlook, but should be conscious of the fact that many Barbadians leave their homeland to seek employment in other parts of the region and the world. It is unquestionable that every national of this land would expect that Barbadians be treated both equally and fairly, when they go in search of job opportunities elsewhere.

In as much as Barbados is committed to the Caribbean Single Market and Economy (CSME), the developments in Barbados provide a real opportunity for the powers that be to act decisively in promoting the idea that labour standards are to be observed. In the movement to CSME, the opportunity is not to be lost to drive home the point that there is no place for the discrimination or exploitation of labour, neither now nor in the future.

> Published: Daily Nation (Newspaper) Monday July 5th, 2004, Page 8; Headlined: 'Migrant Labour Issue'

The Free Movement of Labour

The free movement of Caribbean nationals has been accepted as one of the major aspects to be promoted under the Caribbean Single Market and Economy. In demonstrating its commitment to this ideal, Barbados has taken a more or less lead position, in opening its doors to other CARICOM nationals in search of other employment opportunities. This open door policy has resulted in large numbers of migrant workers being attracted from Guyana.

The net effect of this measure has been the competition that has been created for the declining number of available jobs, particularly in the construction sector. The scores of migrant Guyanese labour that are being brought to this island as contract labour, is said to be occasioned by a shortage of skilled artisans on the island. This claim is a debatable one as there are cries from Barbadian artisans that they have been displaced by virtue of the fact that Guyanese labourers were willing to accept lower rates of pay.

In a contracting economy, where much emphasis is being placed on reduced production costs, it would seem that employers in this sector, have sought to cash in on the opportunity to acquire low cost labour.

This practice is a matter of concern to the local trade union movement, as it serves to compromise the gains it has made, as far as realising a decent base pay for various categories of workers within the construction industry.

Although the trade union movement is committed to the idea of the free movement of labour, it is nonetheless obligated to ensure that the Barbadian labour remains employed, and that it is not discriminated against.

Under Section 4.3 (e) Protocol 1V, the Social Partners agree that national employment policy should specify all, "Seek to protect employment and to provide jobs for those Barbadians who are available for and are desirous of work, to make such work as productive as possible, and to ensure that the freedom of choice of employment in an environment void of any possible form of discrimination where workers have the greatest opportunity to qualify for, and to use their skills and potential in a job well suited to them."

Further the labour movement is committed to protecting the security of tenure of Barbadian labour as provided under Section 4.3 (f) of Protocol 1V, where the Social Partners agree to " Provide adequate safeguards against recourse to contracts of employment for a specific period of time, whose effects are designed to run counter to the purpose of such a policy and so negate the intended protection of workers' security of tenure."

The conclusion may be drawn that the displacement of Barbadian labour forms part of a deliberate policy to weaken the backbone of the local trade union movement. The heart of this apparent orchestrated attack on the local trade union movement may be centred at minimizing union membership. Having achieved this, it provides those unscrupulous employers with a platform from which they could launch their offensive in attempting to change terms and conditions of service, to terms and conditions that are less favourable than those which have been negotiated by the Barbados Workers Union.

Where such practices are evident, this constitutes a serious violation of Section 4.2 of Protocol 1V, on the part of employers. In accordance with this provision, "The Social Partners further agree that such a national employment policy shall seek to give effect at all times to the concept of decent work, as enunciated by the International Labour Organisation."

It becomes seemingly clear that any practices on the part of employers that fall below the accepted Barbadian labour standards can only be described as an attempt to compromise the rights of Guyanese migrant labour, in addition to exploiting them. This apart, the movement remains conscious of the pressure exerted on Barbadian labour, which is challenged to resist negative or backward changes that are being attempted by employers.

It is therefore necessary that the local trade union movement becomes more vigilant and aggressive, as it seeks to protect the rights of labour. The movement must see it as its responsibility to ensure that provisions 4.3 (a) (d) of Protocol 1V are observed.

Section 4.3

(a) Stipulates that the Social Partners agree that such a national employment policy should specifically: "Protect workers and employers who exercise their constitutional right to freedom of association."

(b) Ensure the provision of those conditions which accord with an understanding of the right to do decent work, including a written statement of the particulars of employment , the payment of adequate wages and salaries, reasonable working ties, satisfactory arrangements for wholesome conditions at work, for security when ill or otherwise reasonably absent from work, and for the application of suitable and acceptable benefits on retirement."

It has come to the fore that many businesses who have been awarded construction contracts, and who have sought to import and/or employ Guyanese labour in preference to Barbadian labour, have tended to escape the trade unions by their failure to accord union recognition.

Practices such as these, present a challenge to the labour movement. However, employers who attempt to close their door on trade unions, should heed the caution that the trade union movement is neither dormant nor dead, and will readily reposition itself to meet this challenge.

As Barbados shows its commitment to the free movement of Caribbean people, it can ill afford to lose sight of the severe strain that stands to be imposed on its National Insurance Scheme in meeting payment to unemployment benefits, where there is a high incidence of its nationals being placed on the bread line. Added to this would be the pressure exerted on its various social agencies. Most importantly, the fall out which comes with massive unemployment that is linked to crime and violence and the illicit drug trade cannot be ignored.

Published: Sunday Sun (Newspaper) June 8th, 2003, Page 8A
Headlined: 'Challenges For Trade Unions'

Identifying the Labour Movement's Agenda for 2004

Consistent with the customary practice at the start of the new year, the Congress of Trade Unions and Staff Association of Barbados fittingly extends best wishes to the Government and peoples of Barbados. As the new year dawns, the Congress is mindful of the many challenges which it faced during 2003, yet remaining before it. Not to be deterred, the Congress commits itself to working with the Social Partners, and all other stakeholder interests in bringing about meaningful changes , that are aimed at improving the status of working people, and giving effect to building a better and a more productive Barbadian society.

Continuing on the path of the past year, the Congress pledges to continue the struggle for better working conditions for workers. As it specifically relates to the public service, the Congress will continue to pressure the Government to identify a timetable, towards addressing many of the outstanding non-salary issues that relate to conditions of service. The Congress remains adamant that many of these issues can be addressed, without imposing a financial burden on the treasury. It is our view that Government should act decisively. It would reflect a real commitment to improving the conditions of service under which public servants work. It is imperative that Government sees its response as one meaningful way of addressing the perceived apathy, declining morale and falling productivity levels of the Public Service.

As the ongoing process of upgrading the efficiency of the Public

Service through the Public Sector Reform initiative, the Congress pledges to give support to the process, through working to facilitate ongoing education and training opportunities to both workers and employers. Towards achieving this, CTUSAB will continue to work with the Barbados Workers' Union Labour College, and the National Union of Public Workers' Training Academy. In addition to this, the Congress will undertake to collaborate with the Barbados Employers' Confederation and other stakeholder interests in furthering the cause of worker and employer education.

This apart, Government must adopt a more aggressive approach to Public Sector Reform, and must do so by seeking to upgrade the managerial skills of those in leadership positions and to adequately train staff to be better able to carry out the roles that they are assigned. Since there is no short cut to realising this, CTUSAB will continue to impress on Government the need to treat this initiative, as one of its priorities.

Addressing calls for a more productive Public Service, CTUSAB is forced to concern itself with the slow rate of progress on the part of Government in the computerisation of Government Departments and Agencies.

In undertaking to represent and safeguard the workers' interest, and indeed that of the national good, CTUSAB will closely monitor Government's spending, particular as it relates to wastage on government projects and programmes, excessive spending, the offering of lucrative contracts to foreign consultants and the appointment of Chairpersons to Statutory Boards.

Added to this, it is timely that a call should be made for a review of the progress of the now protracted EDUTECH programme. With the advent of globalization and trade liberalization, and the introduction of the Caribbean Single Market and Economy, the movement now has to remain ever vigilant about preserving the jobs of Barbadians. More over it must review its strategies in dealing with employers who seek to replace Barbadian labour with migrant labour, and at the same time by their actions, seek to compromise the gains relative to the conditions of service, that the labour movement has gained.

As the Congress works towards protecting the rights of workers, it will place on its agenda of priority items, the enactment of the long awaited Employment Rights Bill. Other critical matters which would engage CTUSAB's attention will be the transition process at the Queen Elizabeth Hospital, and the long overdue re-organisation of the ambulance service. CTUSAB considers that Government should move with haste in addressing the transition process at the QEH, towards satisfying all interests that the jobs of the employees are secured, and that their rights and entitlements are intact. Added to the list, CTUSAB will continue to vigorously mount its campaign against supercession in the Public Service.

On the subject of the re-organisation of the ambulance service, Government should now seriously give consideration to this matter, instead of paying lip service to it, inasmuch that it has been on Government's agenda since the mid 1970's. Not only should there be a decisive plan of action to re-organise the ambulance service, but as a priority, Government should seek to have a workable fleet of ambulances in operation, to service the Barbadian public.

> Published: Daily Nation (Newspaper) Thursday January 8th, 2004, Page 8; Headlined: 'CTUSAB Much Still To Do'

Wages and Salaries Negotiations

With General Elections now out of the way, Government has signalled its intention to commence the 2003-2005 Wages and Salaries Revision exercise. Over the years it would seem that Government has focused its attention primarily on the monetary aspect of the negotiations. The history of Public Sector Wages and Negotiations reflects that a number of non-salary items, commonly referred to as conditions of service, remain outstanding following the completion of the exercise.

The fact that the non-salary items/conditions of service form part of the body of proposals submitted to Government by the unions to be considered in the Wages and Salaries agreement there is the expectation that these will be given equal treatment in the negotiations exercise.

The response of Government in not addressing the non-salary items that are included in the wages and salaries proposal is particularly worrisome to the trade union movement, so since some of these have no immediate cost attached to them. The cessation of deductions of the Widows and Children's Fund; lay off not to be counted against an officer in the computation of length of service, removal of asbestos from workplaces- certification to be provided as a condition to return to work, attesting the fact that asbestos has been removed from premises in accordance with the established guidelines, and pension to be a right in law, are examples of such conditions that carry no immediate costs.

In November 2001, the Congress of Trade Unions and Staff Associations of Barbados wrote to the Ministry of the Civil Service to draw its attention to the fact that there were a number of issues outstanding from the 1995, 1997 and 1999 Wages and Salaries Negotiations. In that correspondence, CTUSAB identified a list of forty-eight outstanding items upon which no finality had been reached. Interestingly enough, this was an incomplete listing of outstanding non-salary items.

Accepting that CTUSAB is interested in bringing closure on the outstanding items, it does not remain ignorant of the fact that there is a cost factor attached to the implementation of some of these non-salary items/conditions of service. However, it is equally aware that once an agreement in principle is reached, a timetable can be arrived at, relative to the implementation of each item.

The delay in addressing the non-salary items can serve to do little good towards the motivation of employees, productivity, and enhancing staff morale. Such is defeatist in nature to the efforts of Public Sector Reform, and to the general reformation process that is aimed at bringing the best out of workers, as the island seeks to remain competitive in an age of regional and global competitiveness.

The slow or non response from Government in addressing non salary matters, may be misconstrued to mean that such are not highly placed on Government's priority listing. Additionally, it could be argued that Heads of Department in Government Ministries and Departments have not been using what influence they have to impress upon their superiors the need to address appropriate conditions of service, which would be beneficial to employees within their respective Ministries and Departments, and by extension the wider Public Sector.

The unified approach of negotiations under CTUSAB, has brought with it a measure of success in securing a number of conditions of service, that have benefited employees across the board in the Public Service. One of the most recent of these has been the securing of the Flexibility Allowance in the 2001 - 2003 Wages and Salaries. This in the main applied to Policemen, Fire Officers, Nurses and Prison Officers.

As preparation for the 2003 - 2005 Salary Revision Negotiations commences, CTUSAB remains mindful of the needs of those at the lower end of the salary scale. Conversely, it recognizes that those at the top of the scale must not be denied their due.

It is hoped that Government will bring to the negotiations table an understanding of the difficulty that those at the lower end of the scale faced in coping with the high cost of living in Barbados, when compared to their limited purchasing power. There is the expectation that a speedy conclusion would be reached in upcoming round of negotiations, and that Government will move to address many of the outstanding non-salary items that have been placed before it as part of CTUSAB's body of proposals.

Published: Daily Nation (Newspaper) Monday July 28th, 2003
Headlined: 'CTUSAB Seeks Closure'

Developing a Workplace Crisis Plan

The subject of Occupational Safety and Health has and continues to feature as a main agenda item of the Congress of Trade Unions and Staff Associations of Barbados. CTUSAB has committed itself to a continued programme of worker education, with a view of promoting best workplace safety and health practices, and the general well-being of workers, towards reducing the incidence of illness.

For the most part much emphasis has been placed on occupational health and safety concerns in the workplace, particularly repetitive strain injuries, mental disorder and life threatening disabilities. It is therefore fair to conclude that the focus has been primarily placed on the prevention of workers' loss of productivity, due to disability or illness.

There can be no down playing of the importance attached to following best practice in the workplace as a way towards reducing or eliminating the risk of on the job injury or illness. In as much as this is so, it becomes equally important that workplaces have a known crisis or emergency plan, which should become operable if the need arises.

In Barbados it would seem that our workplace emergency or crisis plan is limited to the boarding up of buildings due on the issuance of a pending of a coming storm or hurricane.

In the past, there was evidence that fire drills were practiced in some of our island's schools, but these are rarely done today. It is about time that Barbados sits up and takes note of some of the disasters which have happened in other parts of the world. If we are to learn from the experience of others, it is important that we move to put systems in place in order to guard against these eventualities. If this is to be taken seriously, it may become necessary to give consideration to statutory regulations that are aimed at ensuring that clear evacuation procedures are established in all work/business places, inclusive of schools, as well as all public places.

In many of our workplaces particularly in the manufacturing/industrialised sector, chemicals and all kinds of hazardous materials are now commonly used. What happens should a disaster strike? Is it enough to only call the Fire Service and the Police?

Have we learnt anything from the fatal accident that occured only a few years ago when a young man lost his life in a fire at one of this island's Industrial Parks? Didn't the recent experience at the Trimart store in Bridgetown serve as a wake up call?

It is important that in Barbados we develop a consciousness with respect to the construction of highrise buildings, as this signals a new building culture, which will mandate the development of accompanying workplace emergency plans.

It is quite noticeable that many of our work places/business houses still have one door entrances and exits. In some places there remains an absence of exit signs. Considering that in most emergencies when all persons must find the nearest exit, it is important that appropriate lighting systems are installed to guide persons to these exits. In the event that the electrical supply is interrupted, or a building becomes smoke filled, such a lighting system would prove to be extremely important.

It is envisaged that this is a new challenge which should engage the attention of the Social Partnership. Indeed a matter of this nature which focuses on the protection of lives of employees and customers, cannot and should not be taken lightly.

Following on the passage of the Safety and Health at Work Act 2005 - 12, it can only be hoped that the policing of our work places, would result in better safety and health practices being observed.

Unpublished Article.

Industrial Harmony

The growing incidence of some wildcat strikes in Barbados has in recent times featured prominently in calling attention to workplace labour disputes. The frequency with which these have tended to surface, communicates a clear message that there is a lack of industrial harmony in workplaces.

This trend is particularly disturbing when one considers that since 1999 there has been an escalation in the number of industrial relations disputes that have been recorded.

Since the second half of 2002 there have been several instances of abrupt work stoppages. In December of that year workers walked off the job at PriceSmart. As the year 2003 dawned, industrial action heightened with work stoppages at the Divi Southwinds Hotel, WIBISCO and at the construction sites of the Barbados Hilton Hotel, the Grantley Adams International Airport and the Crane Beach Hotel.

Of late there have been the Market Workers, Customs Officers and Barbados Water Authority strikes. What is evident is the fact that neither the Public Sector nor the Private Sector has been spared the wrath of industrial action.

The withdrawal of labour has centred around poor working conditions, safety and health concerns, arbitrary dismissal of employees, supercession, generally bad management practices, and poor employer-employee relations, the failure of some employers to recognize a chosen and accredited trade union as the bargaining agent of its employees and the failure on the part of some employers to consult with the trade union when contemplating the introduction of changes that would impact on employees' conditions of service or continued employment. Acknowledging that it is a fundamental right of workers to withdraw their labour, this is not to be taken to mean that wildcat strikes are encouraged or promoted by trade unions. This is not to say that wildcat strikes are to be outlawed.

Where such action is to be taken, as it is necessary in some cases, there is usually a legitimate reason for such. The trade union movement prides itself on following established industrial relations grievance handling procedures, and as a deliberate policy sets out to train its shop stewards in the guiding principles that govern employer/employee relations within the workplace.

When employees are forced to withdraw their labour, this means a loss of productive man-hours. Whereas, the loss of man-hours would be of concern to the labour movement, as it also ought to be to employers, more often than not it is a necessary sacrifice that labour must bear in its own interest.

If maintaining industrial harmony is considered important, then there must be an embracing of the principle as identified by the Social Partners under Section 6.2 of Protocol IV, which reads:

"The Social Partners agree that the maintenance of industrial harmony depends upon the exercise of mutual respect for, and protection of, the rights and entitlements of both employers and workers since they are important elements in achieving the objectives of this Protocol.

(a) Notwithstanding the Employers' right to final decision making and determination to safeguard the viability of their operations, the Social Partners agree that the basis for the protection of the interests and residual rights of said employers are inextricably linked with the programme of the workers and their representatives for the nurturing of a culture of a shared vision with employers for development at the enterprise level.

(b) The Social Partners thus agree that the maintenance of industrial harmony equally demands the safeguarding of the employers' viability, the stability of the government's programme and the security and protection of the workers' tenure, as well as it demands the adoption of the workers and the representatives as important consulting partners in decision making, and in the development of democratic practices at the workplace in furtherance of this objective."

In as much that it is imperative that industrial harmony be maintained in the interest of ensuring that Barbados maintains a sound economy and sustains its competitiveness, it is necessary for all parties to seek to avoid or reduce the potential for labour disputes by recourse to such consultative procedures as may be efficacious; including reference to the Subcommittee of the Social Partners for its advice and the use of its good offices. The labour movement hopes that in the furtherance of the cause of promoting industrial harmony, that all parties will be guided by Section 6.3 of Protocol IV, which stresses that: "The Social Partners also agree that industrial harmony will inevitably be jeopardized if those social protection and social dialogue issues upon which there has been agreement, are thereafter negated by the actions and differing initiatives either of labour, private sector entities or agents of the Government as employer of labour".

A recent analysis completed by the Barbados Employers' Confederation on the subject of 'Wildcat Strikes', concluded that a lack of communication was mainly responsible for workers taking such action.

It is therefore advisable that it would make good sense for employers to take note of this and to act accordingly, for to do otherwise would be to give fuel to the existence of adversarial relations; thus undermining the spirit and intention of the Protocol IV.

Published: Daily Nation (Newspaper) October 8th, 2003 Page 10 A

Worker Recognition

Recognition of the efforts and contributions of workers seems an appropriate approach to be adopted by employers towards motivating workers and creating a level of job satisfaction. The Congress of Trade Unions and Staff Associations of Barbados supports the introduction of any appropriate initiatives that are agreed upon between the workers' representative and the employer towards achieving these ends.

It has been the tendency to concentrate on offering bonus payments to employees, or to identifying an employee of the month or the year. Whereas these measures have realized some results, the question which remains unanswered is: To what extent can it be said that either approach has served as an effective means in motivating employees or enhancing their level of job satisfaction?

If the high incidence of lay-offs, turn over rate of staff and work place labour disputes are anything to go by, it makes it increasingly difficult to understand how these do not impact on any strategies that have been designed to stimulate workers in being more productive and committed to the execution of their various tasks. However, as the nation looks towards creating a more rejuvenated workforce, CTUSAB considers that it is important that all employers begin to consider ways through which they can induce workers to make a difference.

In advocating that greater concentration be placed on worker recognition, CTUSAB urges employers to ensure that they do not miss the mark by virtue of their perception of what worker recognition is all about.

Employers should become cognizant of the fact that it is not simply enough to offer employees incentives, but should ensure that these are linked to achievement.

It is advisable that the reason for any recognition award is known and that the employer communicates the benefit the achievement has brought to the organization. A recognition award for which the criteria is not known, is more than likely to be misconstrued as being given on the basis of favouritism.

It is also important that not only should achievements be recognized but also any action(s) on the part of an employee that leads to the realization of an accomplishment. It therefore it would make good sense if employers sought to recognize the achievements and contributions on a more frequent basis, rather than doing so after long intervals, at which time in some instances, the recognition comes way after the fact, and hence loses its significance. Where this occurs, it certainly does little to inspire employees, and could defeat the purpose for which the recognition award was intended in the first instance.

It would be a matter of being short sighted, if both employers and unions were of the view that worker recognition is primarily linked to bonus payouts. It is our contention that a worker feels recognized where the individual believes that he/she has earned the respect of their superiors at the workplace. This can be a great sense of recognition to be offered to employees, provided that the employer gives them good reason to believe that their services are valued and that they are empowered, by embracing them in the decision-making process of the organization.

CTUSAB contends that effective recognition of employees is attainable, provided that employers demonstrate a willingness to commend and give credit to employees where it is due. Not only should this be done, but it ought to be done in a timely and appropriate manner.

It would certainly be uplifting to employees, if the employer in recognizing the talents and abilities of their various employees based on their achievements and contributions, sought to credit these employees by way of availing them of new opportunities, and/or training towards making a further contribution.

Employers should see the exposing of employees to training as a valuable investment, in as much that it can secure and maintain a cadre of employees who develop a commitment to the organization and provides the basis for a long-term association.

> Published: Daily Nation (Newspaper) Monday October 20th, 2003 Page 17; Headlined: 'Incentives Should Reflect Achievement'

Chapter Two

Trade Unionism - Its Growth and Development

Trade Unionism - A Sense Of Power

Since its emergence out of the struggles of the 1930's, the local trade union movement has played a decisive role in seeking to improve the social and economic well-being of all Barbadians. Further to this, it has been particularly successful in securing significant benefits and conditions of service for employees in both the private and public sectors.

Based on the relatively low percentage of our employed population that is currently unionized, it appears that many seem not to understand how important it is to become unionized. If this is the case, then it is an obvious signal to the local movement that it must aggressively intensify its efforts towards educating members and potential members of the workforce, of the importance attached to being unionized.

The 2001 census indicated that Barbados recorded a population of 269 000. Of this number the labour force stood at 147 000, of which 132 000 were employed. If the latter figure were to be compared against the number of unionized members, it would reflect that less than 30 per cent of the Barbados workforce is unionized.

The picture becomes more dismal considering that of the approximate 27 000 public servants in Barbados, approximately one-fifth is currently unionized. The situation with the private sector is none the rosier, inasmuch that the Barbados Workers Union, which is the largest and virtually the sole private sector union, can boast only of a membership of approximately 20 000 workers. This translates itself into one-seventh of the employed workforce.

Is it to be concluded that the non-unionization of the vast majority is as a result of complacency, apathy or gross indifference? Are there hidden reasons such as the intimidation on the part of some employers, who attempt to deny workers their constitutional right of freedom of association, to be able to join a trade union of choice?

Irrespective of which one of these is a contributory factor, it is important that workers come to recognize that there is strength in numbers. If the workers are to influence decision making that affects their own well-being and that of their families now and in the future, then it ought to be recognized that this can only be achieved through a united front.

It is imperative that workers come to understand that they have a serious responsibility and role to play in promoting and safeguarding their interest. It is certainly not good enough to adopt the attitude that one can sit on the fence and wait, under the guise that the benefits gained through the struggles of the union, will inevitably filter down the line. It would be wise to focus on what more could be achieved if the union, as a body, was able to bring greater pressure to bear by its sheer numerical strength.

Workers are urged not to be shortsighted in terms of how they view the role of the union. It must not be seen as merely a collective bargaining machine. The process of bargaining for wages and salaries and improved conditions of service, is but only part of its overall mandate.

For those who may be in doubt as to the benefits to be derived from being a member of a union, then your attention is called to the fact that apart from developing a sense of power to influence decision making, it offers protection, provides advice, legal representation where appropriate, can serve as a professional body, offers training and opportunities for professional and personal development, and makes available a range of services that are required by members, such as group medical insurance schemes.

Published: Daily Nation (Newspaper) February 21st, 2004
Headlined: 'Unionization'

An Overview of CTUSAB - Its Formation, Role and Achievements

What it is, and what it stands for:

The Congress of Trade Union and Staff Association of Barbados was officially registered as a Trade Union organization in Barbados on August 4th, 1995. This umbrella body was officially launched on Saturday August 12th, 1995 at the BWU - 'Solidarity House.'

The initial step towards developing a formal structure emerged out of a meeting convened at Solidarity House on September 29th, 1991. At this meeting a ten member grouping made up of Trade Unions and Staff Associations, took the decision to organize themselves under the name of the Coalition of Trade Unions and Staff Associations of Barbados.

The formation of the Coalition was considered in some quarters as a 'loose arrangement. This view emerged out of the perception that the Coalition was not a legally constituted body, and hence functioned merely as a collaborative body. There can be no denying that it did not have a formal constitution, and hence the claim had some validity.

It was not until February 28th, 1992, that a sub-committee was set up to commence work on a draft constitution. The reality is that it took virtually another three years before the final document was completed. The constitution was accepted at a meeting of July 12th, 1995.

In an attempt to organize the functioning of the Coalition, an Interim Executive was put in place. Bro. Leroy Trotman - General Secretary of the BWU was identified as the Chairman, with Keith Yearwood - the then President of the NUPW as the Co-Chairman.

For the first decade of its existence, the Congress remained under the able leadership of Comrade Senator Sir Leroy Trotman. In 2006, some thirteen organizations were affiliated to CTUSAB. The newest members to the grouping are the Nurses Assistants and Aides Association of Barbados and Association of Principals of Public Primary Schools.

The founding members of CTUSAB were:

- The Barbados Workers Union
- The National Union of Public Workers
- The Barbados Union of Teachers
- The Barbados Secondary Teachers Union
- The Police Association
- The Fire Service Association
- The Prison Officers Association
- The Barbados Registered Nurses Association
- The Barbados Association of Medical Practitioners
- Barbados Association of Principals of Public Secondary Schools

The Sugar Industry Supervisors Association, now renamed the Sugar Industry Staff Association (SISA), was the latest organization to join the umbrella body when it operated under the name of the Coalition. It was accepted into membership in October 1991. This was subsequent to the inaugural meeting in September, when the decision was taken by unions and staff associations to form themselves into a collaborative body, for the express purpose of formulating a response to Government planned initiatives to rescue the ailing economy.

The road to the consolidation of the labour organizations under one umbrella was not without some alarm. It received an early threat, when in May 1993; the Barbados Association of Medical Practitioners (BAMP) withdrew from the Coalition. BAMP cited its dissatisfaction with the failure of the Coalition's leadership to adopt BAMP's mandate, which called for the resignation of the then Prime Minister, Rt. Honourable Erskine Sandiford.

The Congress of Trade Unions and Staff Associations of Barbados has emerged as a respected voice of Barbados labour, as it represents the collective views of its members on broad national issues of an Industrial Relations, Socio-Economic and Political nature.

As an umbrella organization, CTUSAB seeks to strengthen the labour movement by positioning itself towards influencing policy decisions that impact on workers and the populace at large.

It is to be recognized that the work of the Congress is not limited to the national front, but extends to address regional and global issues that impact on civil rights and liberties; including human rights and trade human rights, which all people must enjoy.

The focus of the Congress is clearly set out in the aims and objectives of its constitution: For example the constitution specifically speaks to:

1. Promoting the interests of its members, and generally to advance the social and economic welfare of the workers of Barbados.

2. The securing of legislation, which will safeguard and improve the economic security and social welfare of workers, and the security and welfare of all people.

3. Promoting the cause of peace and freedom in the world, and assisting and cooperating with free and democratic labour movements throughout the world.

4. Promoting and improving inter union harmony, and establishing a framework for the resolution of disputes.

It is significant to note that the constitution also provides for the sovereignty of each of its affiliates to be respected. This is reflected under the aims and objectives of the constitution, which speak specifically to promoting and respecting the autonomy of each affiliate.

Evidence that this has been observed, is recorded in the Congress's acceptance of the NUPW decision to undertake to negotiate separately with Government, in arriving at a two year wages and salaries agreement. The fact that a representative of CTUSAB and the NUPW respectively are present at each other's negotiations sessions with Government, remains as a living testimony of CTUSAB's respect for individual sovereignty and autonomy. It is important to point out, that the Congress holds steadfastly to the promotion of democratic ideals. It is also equally important to note that CTUSAB remains free of any partisan political affiliation.

How is the CTUSAB managed?

The management of CTUSAB is entrusted to an Executive Board of Directors. There are seven elected officers. These are: a President, 1st Vice President, 2nd Vice President, 3rd Vice President, General Secretary, Assistant General Secretary and Treasurer, who are elected at the Biennial Conference of the organization. A representative of each affiliate also sits on the Board of Directors. The Biennial Conference appoints an auditor and three trustees.

Dues payable by each affiliate are used to fund the operations of CTUSAB. The dues paid by each affiliate are calculated on the basis of declared membership. It is important to note that CTUSAB receives no funding by way of a subvention from Government.

The declared membership of an affiliate is also used as a means in determining the number of delegates each affiliate is entitled to have seated at the Biennial Conference.

Immediate factors which contributed to the formation of CTUSAB

The formation of the Congress dates back to the 1991 economic crisis in Barbados. It came at a time when the island was faced with a major fiscal deficit. The extent and nature of the crisis necessitated that the Government introduce a number of measures, aimed at reducing expenditure, whilst at the same time increasing its revenue base.

A brief review of the situation at the time reveals that Government sought to acquire a standby loan of US $28 million. It also sought to access funds to the tune of US $27.7 million from the Compensatory Contingency Financing Facility.

Tied to the IMF loan were a number of conditions. In meeting the conditions of the loan, Government identified a set of stringent policy measures. These included a reduction in expenditure, increased taxation, the removal of tax concessions and a freeze on basic wages and salaries for a period of two years. On July 31st, 1991 the then Prime Minister, The Rt. Hon. Lloyd Erskine Sandiford, invited the leadership of all trade unions and Staff Associations to a meeting to discuss the difficulties facing the economy. It was at this meeting that the nature and extent of the problem became more apparent to trade union leaders.

The conditions tied to the IMF loan were to become a source of worry to the labour movement. The implications for labour were horrific. The labour movement was quick to recognize that any reduction in Government's wages and salaries bill, effectively translated itself into massive layoffs and/or redundancies within the Public Sector. It painted a picture of great social dislocation and hardship.

The need for the trade union leaders to consolidate a position on this matter was accentuated by the suggestions that a devaluation of the Barbados dollar was being contemplated.

At a meeting on August 8th 1991, under the chairmanship of Comrade Leroy Trotman, a unified position was reached by the forty-six persons in attendance who were representatives of the grouping made up of four unions and six Staff Associations. The commitment to a unified approach to the crisis was demonstrated when the Coalition publicly voiced support for a demonstration organized by the NUPW on September 23rd 1991.

The role and achievements of the CTUSAB

CTUSAB must be credited for its efforts in forging the development of the social partnership of Barbados. The tripartite approach to governance, was a major development to come out of the 1991 crisis.

The economic turbulence set the stage for the unions and staff associations to come together under an umbrella body. It could also be said that this might have influenced the private sector to organize itself under an umbrella body, known as the Private Sector Agency.

In response to the economic crisis the trade union movement advanced that negotiations should be initiated with Government, with a view of developing a package based on alternatives to any reduction in wages and salaries. The majority of the seventeen specific proposals put to Government presented sacrifices as a part of labour's contribution to the required stabilisation programme. The basis of Labour's response was to save jobs.

This forced a response from both Government and the Private Sector. In the final analysis, history was created when the trade union movement, Government and the Private Sector came together to initiate dialogue on how best to deal with the national problems and issues of economic importance. The result of this was the Prices and Income Protocol 1, which was signed on August 24th, 1993. The significance of Protocol 1 was that it sought to maintain the existing parity in the rate of exchange of the Barbados dollar. To the credit of the Labour movement, successive Protocols have been signed in 1993, 1995, 1998 and on May Day of 2002.

Official opening of CTUSAB's 5th Biennial Conference, September 22, 2004
From left: Dennis de Peiza, General Secretary, right: Verneta Durant, President, NAAAB

The action of the labour movement, which accounted for the development of the tripartite approach to governance on the island, paved the way for ongoing consultation to take place through the Sub Committee of the Social Partnership. This Committee, meets monthly to discuss labour related matters and other important national issues.

Overall, CTUSAB has recorded achievements which can be described as phenomenal. Its existence and status are recognized nationally. It now has representation at various levels. For example, it is now represented on the Board of Management of this island's Government Secondary Schools. It is also represented on the National Insurance Board, the Tripartite Technical Sub Committee of the Central Bank, The National Committee for Monitoring the Rights of the Child, The Performance Review and Development Committee (PRDS), and the Board of Directors of the Queen Elizabeth Hospital, just to name a few.

At a higher level, the Congress now meets with delegations from various international bodies such as the International Monetary Fund and International Labour Organization. Further, it engages consultants whose services are acquired by Government for one purpose or another. It meets with Ministries and Departments of Government to address various labour issues, ranging from matters of an administrative nature to proposed legislation. The work of the Congress towards national development is reflected in its Policy Statement.

This document covers a range of issues such as the national debt, regional integration, privatisation, consumer protection, globalisation, penal reform and land use. CTUSAB has led the way in many instances. For example, it has sought to address the issue of HIV/AIDS in the work place, by producing a policy document on the subject. Government has since endorsed the work done by the Congress, in developing a National Policy on HIV/AIDS.

It is CTUSAB that is to be credited for advancing the idea of a 100% Bajan Buy Local Campaign. This idea was conceptualized as a means of promoting the employment of Barbadian labour, through the consumption of local products.

CTUSAB has been in the vanguard of influencing major national changes. It is to maintain a focus on the protection of the rights of workers to freedom of association, and to the recognition of trade unions by employers. One of its significant achievements in this regard, was the push for amendment of the Law, to ensure the right of Police, Prison and Fire Officers to freedom of association, thus allowing them to enjoy full membership of CTUSAB.

CTUSAB has remained worker centred in all of its actions. At the forefront of what it seeks to accomplish, is the creation of better working conditions and improved wages and salaries for workers.

CTUSAB has won a number of improved benefits for workers. These include:

- Pension as a right in law

- Bank Holiday pay for part time teachers who are denied work when a work day is lost.

- A flexibility allowance for Prison, Fire and Police Officers and Nurses.

- Compensation for Police, Fire and Prison Officers injured or killed in the line of duty.

- Amendment to the Law to allow for freedom of association, where by the Police, Prison and Fire Officers to allow personnel to enjoy full membership of CTUSAB.

Teacher Unions and Challenges in Education

*President's Address to the Annual Conference
of the Barbados Union of Teachers
Grand Barbados Hotel April 7th, 1998*

I welcome the opportunity today to address this 24th Annual Conference of this Union. Having reflected in an objective manner on the work of this organization over the past year, I feel obliged to share with you some of my thoughts and concerns, and to do so by focusing on the level of progress that has been made. In addition, I will speak to what, in my opinion, needs to be done to further the cause of the Barbados Union of Teachers.

The past year has indeed been active, busy and challenging. The Union has had to respond to issues at every turn. It is significant to note that it has maintained its vigilance on matters pertaining to education and has worked assiduously to safeguard the rights of teachers in the workplace, to acquire improvements in working conditions, to negotiate the best salaries increases for its members, as well as to agitate for reforms in education which are in the best interest of the system.

Overall, tremendous success has been recorded, of which this Union ought to be justly proud. I would however caution that amidst this success, there is no room for complacency, for there is much work yet to be done.

It would be foolhardy not to be cognizant of the fact that matters such as Edutech 2000, Teacher Appraisal and Public Sector Reform remain agenda items, which the B.U.T will seriously have to address during the ensuing year.

As the teachers' unions prepare to forge ahead in meeting the new challenges in Education, the B.U.T. as a single entity, remains mindful of the need to have a closer networking with the major interest in Education.

The union is therefore supportive of adopting the tripartite approach that embraces the teachers' unions, the Ministry of Education and the Parent Teachers' Association, as they work together in developing new policy initiatives and approaches in Education. The importance of dialogue, consultation and collaboration must be stressed, as these provide a medium through which clear understandings can be reached, if the best intentions of promoting and enhancing the delivery of education to our nation's children, are to be manifested beyond the conceptualization stage.

It is therefore important that we all recognize the significance of the theme of this year's conference, "The Role of the Teacher Trade Unions and the Social Partnership in meeting the new challenges in Education."

I will however not attempt to elaborate further on the theme, but will leave it into the competent hands of our guest speaker, Mr. Evelyn Greaves, whom we can expect to elucidate at will. You can be assured Sir, that you will have our undivided attention when you rise to address this 24th Annual Conference.

Permit me at this point to momentarily revisit the episode played out at last year's Annual Conference, which focused on the issue of representation. This gave rise to some rancour and division and was potentially devastating as far as the image of this union was concerned.

The potential fallout has been arrested through the positive work of the outgoing executive committee, our efforts have done much to restore confidence in the organization and strengthen the bond of unity within the ranks.

I can assure you that this Union has not only responded to every call for assistance but has been meticulous in its follow up, as it sought to provide quality service to members.

It is important at this stage that I thank the general membership for the strong support it has given to the executive committee. It must be pointed out that members kept constant vigil over developments in their workplaces and education in general, and have provided unlimited information, which has assisted the executive in the planning and coordination of its efforts and strategies.

This suggests to me that the call for the membership to remain vigilant has not gone unheeded.

Let me now turn my attention to one of the major challenges that presented itself throughout the course of the year. The inordinate high number of grievances which came to the fore, has given cause for concern, particularly since many of those reported identified poor management practices and poor management and employee relations as the core of the problem.

Our investigations revealed that some principals have failed in following procedure in completing adverse reports on teachers. The sad reality is that there has often been the lack of supporting evidence brought to collaborate charges laid by some principals. More often than not the problem between the Principal and teachers seem to have its genesis in the poor personal relationship between the two parties.

It is no longer appropriate to appoint persons to the post of principal based on years' experience as a teacher, and on the level of academic qualifications.

Emphasis needs to be placed on managerial and interpersonal skills, if our system is to be better served.

It is therefore a challenge to the authorities to select persons to manage our schools, who demonstrate initiative and a will to lead, and who are conscious of the importance of following a collective approach to management.

This Union strongly views that if these suggestions are taken on board, then the general quality of leadership at the hierarchy of schools could be enhanced.

I suggest that principals and persons aspiring to such office should develop the four main qualities as identified by educators Hellriegel and Woodman.

These qualities to which I refer are, developing visionary skills (i.e.

to have the skills to pull people towards them), to have the skill to effectively communicate with others, to be able to recognize one's own strengths and weaknesses, and most importantly, to develop the skill of sharing power with subordinates.

This means that the principal as a leader should provide opportunities for members of staff to share in developing strategies. This approach is deemed to be the most appropriate, as it would identify with the fact that effective leaders are not dictators but are sensitive to the needs of others.

On the subject of maintaining good professional relationship amongst our teachers, and administrators, I would want to remind teachers of the need to observe some degree of loyalty to the administration of the school.

Equally so, principals who by their actions reflect that they are persons of integrity would merit the respect and loyalty of staff. It is therefore unethical for a principal to make an unfavourable report, whether written or oral, on a teacher without first informing that teacher of his/her intentions, and the contents of the intended report.

If these were observed, it would augur well for developing better management employee relations in our schools. In focusing on the subject of the discipline of teachers, the B.U.T. has pointed out for some time now that there is the need for a Teacher Service Commission, under whose jurisdiction complaints brought against teachers would fall. Mindful of this, the Union welcomes the recent announcement by the Hon, Minister of Education, (re. Weekend Nation Newspaper, February 13, page 18A under the headline "Education Ministry's Role to Change.")

"During the course of this year, you will see the Ministry establishing a complaints committee that will seek to take Educational and parental complaints out of the realm of the technical section and political elements."

However, I must caution that it would be unwise not to include the teachers unions as part of this committee.

Further, it is the hope that this committee would comprise of persons from 'appropriate backgrounds', who have requisite skills and competencies. It would be desirable if there were consultation with the teachers unions prior to the appointment of this committee.

I will now turn my attention to the burning issues of security, indiscipline and violence at schools.

In the main, many of the island's primary schools remain as open thoroughfares. This provides easy access to members of the general public. Many of our schools continue to be burglarized and vandalized by persons in the community at will.

Teachers and students now go about their business in a less than supposedly comfortable environment. Teachers are often subjected to verbal abuse, threats and harassment while on the job from unknown persons, and even some of those who are said to be at the school on legitimate business.

It has now gone to the extreme, where we find individuals coming directly off the street into the classroom. The events of February 18th at the St. Giles Composite School, which left a student badly beaten, tell the tale.

There can be no doubt that teachers and students are at serious risk and the school can no longer be regarded as a safe haven.

The problem of security at our schools seems not to be seriously addressed. The membership of this union now ought to see this as a fundamental issue on which some firm position must be reached and be prepared to guide and support the Executive Committee in a plan of action to get a positive response.

I suggest that the B.U.T. has to see a resolution to this matter before the start of the 1998-99 academic year in September. I contend that the local authority has a responsibility toensure that all students and teachers have access to schools that are safe, orderly and drug free, and that students and staff are able to learn and work in schools that have clear disciplinary codes.

Considering the latter, the question of indiscipline and violence in schools should not escape our attention. The Union has a serious responsibility to take a look at emerging negative trends in our schools and to join forces with the Ministry of Education in coming up with ideas and strategies in an effort to counteract them.

It is my opinion that there are too many children who are on the streets of Barbados as a result of being suspended or expelled from school for acts of indiscipline.

I consider the system to be flawed, if it provides an escape route for our students from the classroom. I know for a fact that between 19 and 24 February lists appeared on the notice board of a secondary school with the names of 24 students who were suspended from school in that one-week. The union must therefore remain in the forefront in lobbying for the removal of stringent measures in the

Education Act, which constrain teachers in being able to discipline students.

The fear of litigation ought not to remain hanging over our heads, as a deterrent to the discipline of students.

The political directorate and other relevant social agencies must refocus their attention on the drastic moral decline in our society and in so doing, examine the impact it has had on life in our schools.

We must recognize that based on current trends, teachers are fast losing the battle of control over children. We must fight to ensure that students do not gain the ascendancy over teachers. To leave this situation as it stands is to concede that the role of the school as an institution of socialization, is quickly diminishing. We must restore dignity within our schools and not simply pass the buck in proportioning blame for the growing indiscipline and indifference, which now characterize our schools.

Permit me now to focus on the success stories of this Union for the year under review. I draw your attention to the following:

1. Twenty-eight teachers have been appointed to established posts in the Primary Schools.

2. Some progress has been made in having the 103 vacant posts at Secondary Schools filled. Our information suggests that to date approximately one-third of these posts have been filled.

3. Agreement has been reached for provision to be made for protective clothing for teachers in technical areas at secondary schools.

4. Through its persistent efforts the Union has seen the re-commencement of the two-year Teachers' Training Programme at Erdiston College.

5. The Union has made successful representation to the Ministry of Education for improved conditions at a number of schools. The extensive works completed at Carrington's and the St. Philip Primary Schools in particular, hold immense significance for the union, since the major repair and refurbishing work undertaken justified the strong positions that this Union took.

6. This year a Counseling and Support Services Education Training Programme has been launched for members of the Union. Efforts are on-going to source funding to support the setting up of a Professional Counseling and Support Service Programme, which would be freely accessible to all members.

7. Significant progress has been made in resolving a number of outstanding individual grievances, some dating back into the early 1990's.

8. The Union has attracted a number of new members and has seen the renewal of membership of some who had previously withdrawn their association with the organization.

9. Work is ongoing in reaching a resolution to the manner of how transfers are completed in our schools. As you would recall this was the source of some difficulties for this Union at the start of the current school year.

   The B.U.T. and the B.S.T.U. have started negotiations with the

Ministry of Education towards arriving at a Memorandum of Understanding.

One of the proposed features of this agreement would be to have written notices served of pending transfer, to be followed by an agreed period of time that should elapse before the transfer becomes effective.

10. The Union has successfully negotiated for the appointment of Clerk/Typists in the Primary Schools. As of January 16 such persons have been appointed to serve schools across the island.

With regards to the recently concluded salary negotiations, the B.U.T. must be proud of the achievement of the 9.25 per cent settlement, which just about realized the instructions of its members to conclude a wage settlement at a minimum of 10 per cent over the two-year period.

The Union in continuing to realize benefits for its members at the bargaining table and is close to finalizing a two-year salary agreement for the staff of the St. Gabriel's School. A feature of this agreement in principle has already been reached on this matter.

11. This union has strongly resisted any attempt by the Ministry of Education to introduce a Teacher Appraisal Instrument in any form, without negotiation.

Further, our efforts have ensured that there is nothing in the framework for the proposed programme of institutional appraisal, which compromises the Union's position on

Teacher Appraisal.

I am sure that members would be pleased to know that the Executive Committee has fulfilled its mandate and is in a position to present to this Conference, reports from those Special Committees set up to look at creating the position for a paid officer, a review of the constitution, the decentralization of balloting, and plans for the use of the property at Waterford.

I now leave you to judge whether this Executive Committee under my leadership, has delivered. I suggest to you that we do not seek to turn back the hands of the clock but continue to go forward, riding high on the wave of a new vision.

As we look ahead to the ensuing year, I would want to suggest some areas on which this Union needs to focus. Primarily, matters pertaining to the Union's finances ought to be given priority. Based on the nature of the debate that followed the presentation of the Annual Audited Financial Statement, I believe that a call for review of the management of the union finances is in order.

It is my considered opinion that this union cannot continue to function without a Finance Committee. This seems to me to be an integral part of the operations of any modern day national organization. There is the need to develop our financial base through identifying a comprehensive approach towards the recruitment of new members. There is a need to tap into the 400-600 non-unionized members in our primary and secondary school system. Clearly our approach to membership recruitment needs to be more aggressive.

Further, consideration ought to be given to securing from

Government an annual subvention for the purpose of financing training programmes.

In an effort to make the full resources available to members, emphasis has to be placed on developing a resource centre at the union. It is embarrassing that after years of talking, the union has failed to organize the volume of literature of all sorts, which have been made available to it for use by members and students at various institutions, who frequently request information for research purposes.

It is critical that the Union fights to ensure that equal privileges and benefits are provided for teachers in the primary schools. For example why should the start of the school year for primary schools be scheduled for Mondays and secondary schools on Tuesdays?

Why should secondary schools be closed for the finals of the Barbados Secondary Schools' Athletic Championships, while Primary Schools remain opened for the Barbados Union of Teachers Primary School Championship?

Why is there a limited number of specialists Physical Education teachers in our primary schools? Why should only one placement be allocated to teachers at the primary level to pursue the Dip. Ed. Programme at Erdiston College?

As this term of office comes to an end, let me thank the media for the excellent support given throughout the year, which did much to keep the work of this union to the fore; in addition to boosting the image of the organization.

To you the members of the outgoing executive committee, do accept my thanks for the tremendous support you have given throughout the year.

Let me pay special tribute to our General Secretary Ms. Undene Whittaker for her commitment and dedication to the call of duty.

I extend congratulations to those members of the outgoing executive committee who have been returned to office unopposed, and wish all other candidates good luck at the polls.

Finally, I will return to the theme of the Conference, only to restate this B.U.T's continued commitment to the social partnership, recognizing the importance attached to it, in meeting the challenges in Education.

We urge that the notion of respect for each other and goodwill will characterize the relationship, which exists amongst the stakeholders in Education.

Distinguished guests, ladies and gentlemen thank you for your presence this morning, and I do look forward to a successful conference."

B.U.T Flaunts Proud Record

As the Barbados Union of Teachers celebrates its 30th Anniversary as an independent trade union, there can be no doubt that this institution in its short history has made a tremendous contribution to the development of the teaching profession and to education policy formulation in Barbados

Since it was established as an independent body on May 27, 1974, this union can proudly boast of an excellent track record, which can be associated with the progressive and visionary leadership that it has attracted during the years of its existence.

To date eleven individuals have served in the office of president of this distinguished organization. These include the late John Cumberbatch, who became the union's first president, Marjorie Marshall, John Lovell, Desmond Browne, Victor Hutchinson, Jeff Broomes, Ronald Jones, Dennis de Peiza, Harry Husbands, Undene Whittaker and the incumbent Karen Best.

In its formative years, the BUT was seen in the eyes of many as a radical organization, whose intention it would seem was directed towards influencing sweeping changes in the delivery of education, education policy formulation and improvements in the conditions of service of teachers.

Over the years the BUT has remained committed to the cause by challenging the administration of the educational system towards ensuring that high standards are maintained in the delivery of education and the formulation of educational policies. This apart, it is known for its consistent efforts towards uplifting the image and status of the teaching profession, through its perpetual struggles to secure improved conditions of service for teachers.

The assertion that the BUT emerged as a radical organization seemingly grew out of the strong views articulated by John Cumberbatch (1974-1979). History would recall that on the subject of zoning as it related to the system of transfer from primary to secondary school, the then President John Cumberbatch was quoted as having said, "There would be no Common Entrance Examination. Pupils would move automatically from Primary to Secondary School."

Strong and vibrant leadership has remained a feature of the BUT since its broke away from the Civil Service Association, which was formerly a division of the National Union of Public Workers. As a matter of fact it was under the dynamic leadership of Carl Springer (1969-73) who led the BUT grouping then a division of the Civil Service Association, that the struggle for the independence of the BUT was initiated.

As we reflect the BUT can be proud of the fact that it has produced a cadre of quality leaders, all of whom have gone on to make significant contributions in other spheres at the national and regional level.

Apart from that the BUT can proudly boast of many from amongst its ranks who now find themselves in key positions of responsibility at the national level. The distinguished list of names include the Hon. Reginald Farley, Minister of Education, Youth Affairs and Sports, the Hon. Cynthia Forde, Minister of State in The Ministry of Education, Youth Affairs and Sports, the Hon. Rawle Eastmond,

Minister of Labour and Social Security, the Hon. Gline Clarke, the Minister of Public Works, Ronald Jones, Opposition Member of Parliament, and Harry Husbands, Executive Director, Barbados Employers Confederation.

Some of those recognizable names that have been called to higher service within the Ministry of Education are, Glenroy Cumberbatch, Deputy Chief Education Officer, Idmay Denny, Deputy Chief Education Officer, Dan Carter, Senior Education Officer and C. Walter Harper, Director of EDUTECH Programme.

Added to this are the names of some members who have served the Union in various capacities and who have received appointments to the post of Principal or Deputy Principal in both primary and secondary schools. These include, Grantley Osbourne, Sydwin Bayne, Bradston Clarke, Bertram Murray, Victor Hutchinson, Karen Best, Barbara Smith, Jeff Broomes, Cobin Hinds, Catherine Jordan, David Catlyn, Matthew Farley and Marcia Graham.

It is fair to conclude that the BUT, as a professional organization, has through the exposure given to those who have served it, has contributed to their overall development. It is to the credit of BUT that the majority of those who have moved to higher level of service, have not parted company but retained their membership with the union.

Having identified some of the positives associated with the BUT, it is equally important that some attention is focused on the major drawbacks that present immediate challenges to the union. A seemingly fall-off in the once pronounced vibrancy that characterized the union must be a growing cause for concern.

Despite the fact that there continues to be some semblance of a vocal leadership, it however seems that the membership has lapsed into some level of complacency. If the ground covered and gains made over the past 30 years are not to be eroded, then it is important that the membership be encouraged by way of carefully planned strategies, to become more involved in the life of the union.

To begin with there must be the resuscitation of an active stewards body. The declining membership of the union appears to be another grey area, which the leadership must become proactive in addressing. Inasmuch that the teaching profession has a direct source of potential members, the union must aggressively pursue each individual who remains not unionised. As BUT looks towards the future, the future leadership ought to address the level of fragmentation within its ranks if the stability of the union is not to be compromised. It seems pointless to have three or four groupings emerging out of the teaching service under the banner of staff associations, purporting to represent sectorial interest. Based on their sherr numerical strength, these associations are limited in attempting to stand on their own.

The BUT would best be encouraged to address the idea of establishing divisions within its ranks, and to use this approach as the platform to address groups concerns where appropriate. Not disrespecting the right of any legally constituted grouping to form a union or association under the law of the land, this could be examined as a viable option to be pursued as a means of arresting the emerging trend, which to all intents and purposes, does not serve the best interest of the profession.

Article Published: Barbados Union of Teachers 'Outlook Magazine'.

Concerns About Failing System

The Caribbean Union of Teachers recently concluded its 29th Biennial Conference in Barbados. As anticipated, the subjects of violence in schools, maintaining quality teaching standards, the rapid turnover of teachers and the diminishing supply of male educators in Caribbean schools, all featured prominently in the one-week-long discussions.

It would be a gross error of judgement if the assumption was drawn that these problems were unique to the Caribbean. As if to dismiss this as a totally misguided notion, the 1999 Annual Representative Assembly of the National Education Association of the United States of America (NEA) held in Orlando, Florida, in the month of July, sought to address these and other pertinent issues that have emerged in education. It is important to note that the current challenges will undoubtedly surface amongst those, which educators will continue to face at the start of the new millennium.

Presently, there is some public concern that the education system has been failing. Arguably there is merit in this contention, if only from the point of view that the system has been forced to keep pace with the rapid changes within education and the world at large. Consistent with these constant changing trends, would be the urgent need to improve on current teaching standards, in order to ensure that quality education is continually delivered.

It should therefore become apparent that quality teacher preparation programmes ought to be developed. This points to the fact that there is a need to equip teachers with the required skills to meet the demands placed on them, in servicing the educational needs of students. It should however be noted that in addition to quality teacher preparation programmes, there is the need to provide equipment, materials and resources to compliment the skills which teachers acquire, if effective teaching and learning is to take place.

On this subject of improved quality teaching standards, the Orlando Sentinel of July 1, 1999 published the following statement made by Mr. Bob Chase, president of the National Education Association:

"The public is ready to acknowledge teachers as a solution, not a problem . . . The Union has pushed for more mentoring of new teachers and national certification as ways of improving the stock of teachers . . . Teacher quality is 'Front and centre' of the Union's efforts to improve education."

In underscoring the need for improvements to effect quality teaching standards, President Chase stated, "Teachers must contend with rising standards, the technology explosion and students who are harder to reach than ever. To stay at the top of their profession, teachers must constantly reinvent themselves and seek new skills."

With the increasing pressures being placed on teachers, the educational system is the poorer for it. In the main, the burn out syndrome has begun to impact greatly on teachers. The result of this is an exodus of teachers from the system. It is therefore anticipated that this issue and others such as the mentoring of teachers, the lack of respect for the overall profession, large class sizes, inadequate pay for teachers in an open market where skills can attract higher salaries, the feminization of the teaching profession, and the challenges facing male teachers leading to their withdrawal from the profession, will engage the attention of teacher trade unionists in the Caribbean and beyond.

One challenge which needs to be thoroughly addressed is that of attracting and maintaining new teachers in the profession. It is now apparent that the large number of teachers retiring or leaving the profession has swollen the ranks of beginning teachers. It is now vital, more so than ever before, to provide training for new teachers before they enter the classroom.

According to Janet Gless, associate director of the New Teacher Centre of the University of California in Santa Cruz, "We have dropped teachers in a sink or swim induction, we can't do that anymore".

Bob Chase, president of the NEA concurred with the view that training for new teachers was a major challenge. On this subject, the Orlando Sentinel, July 07, 1999, quoted Chase as having said: "Schools must do more to ease new teachers in the profession. Too often first year teachers are assigned to the toughest schools and isolated from other teachers, with little or no mentoring. It is no wonder that twenty per cent of teachers leave the profession after one year, and half of the teachers in urban schools within five years."

As we enter into a new millennium it is indeed a challenge for teachers in the Caribbean to find solutions to the challenges which confront the delivery of education in our schools throughout the region.

Most importantly, the Caribbean Union of Teachers and individual Teacher Trade Unions across the region must take the lead in influencing education policy. This is paramount to their efforts, if meaningful changes in education are to be realized, and the teacher trade union movement is to earn the respect it deserves.

Published: Daily Nation (Newspaper) September 20, 1999
Headlined: 'Concerns About Failing System'

Workers' Rights Under Attack

Trade Union leaders throughout the Caribbean should take careful note of the recent statements attributed to Mr. Basdeo Panday, Prime Minister of Trinidad and Tobago, and his Minister of Education, Dr. Nanan.

The words of Mr. Panday that "Any teacher who abandons his students is a criminal and should be treated as such", are appalling and certainly unbecoming of a Caribbean statesman and leader of his state.

What makes his statement so damning, is the fact that Mr. Panday was a noted trade union leader, who must be credited as being fully knowledgeable of the legitimate means available to trade unions to remonstrate their causes.

If it was accepted that Mr. Panday's statement was a result of a hasty response, surely the statement attributed to Education Minister Nanan suggested that the Government of Trinidad and Tobago seemingly holds a common position relative to their perception of the rights of workers to publicly demonstrate the particular cause.

Minister Nanan was adamant that those teachers who went on strike would be reported to the Teaching Service Commission and disciplinary action would be taken against them.

It seems therefore, that the right to strike is being outlawed in Trinidad and Tobago. Are we seeing a growing trend in the Caribbean, where the political directorates have lost their respect for the rights of workers, and by extension, their obvious regard for the labour movement?

One would have thought that we have long outlived the era of the Forbes Burnham regime in Guyana. Back then, our Caribbean leaders were quick to condemn his vile forms of behaviour, which oppressed working class people. Many a voice then was raised to call attention to the violation of human rights and justice.

If Caribbean leaders today are supportive of a democratic system of Government and respect the I.L.O. Conventions on the rights of workers, then, it is the responsibility of our leaders to condemn the statement made by their colleague, Mr. Panday.

The wider Caribbean labour movement ought to respond to such a damaging statement from Mr. Panday, for it has the potential of being cancerous.

There is ample evidence to suggest that trends are easy to follow in the Caribbean, and hence no stone should be left unturned to ensure that this particular seed does not develop.

The labour movement has to ensure that such a threat to the rights of workers and to the movement itself does not emerge. The Caribbean Union of Teachers, in particular, needs to speak out.

The teaching profession throughout the Caribbean is seemingly under siege. Teachers and public servants generally have now become the scapegoats of their employers. The struggle for better salaries and conditions of service, seem to be never ending.

Complacency must not set in, and therefore the labour movement needs to remain entrenched in the battle, despite the vicious attacks and efforts to weaken and destabilize it.

The Trinidad & Tobago Unified Teachers Association (TTUTA) must be complimented on the firm stance taken and must be encouraged to continue the struggle, recognizing that their cause is a fair and just one.

Published: Barbados Sunday Advocate September 15th, 1996

Chapter Three

Problems In Education

World Congress on Teaching

During the month of July 1998 I had the distinct privilege of attending the Second World Congress of Education International in Washington, D.C. It was an interesting experience from the point of view that more than 2 000 teachers from 150 nations gathered in one place to share their opinions on matters affecting the teaching profession.

At the end of the Congress, it was evident that teachers across the globe shared similar problems and recognized the importance of working together by way of calling the attention of governments and all relevant world bodies by way of resolutions passed, to the concerns and struggles of the teaching profession.

On the subject of child labour, a resolution was passed condemning governments that failed to legislate comprehensively or act decisively against child labour, as well as employers who exploited children to increase profits.

The Congress called on member units to cooperate with Education International, and through it with ICFTU, ILO, UNICEF, UNESCO, other Trade Unions, union centers and Non Governmental Organizations at the national level, to eliminate child labour nationally, regionally and internationally.

With respect to the status of teachers, the resolution passed called for the improvement of all teachers worldwide and urged education authorities, governments and inter-governmental organizations to ensure that teachers have an adequate working environment, including the technology and the resources necessary for teaching.

The resolution identified that a conducive working environment would be considered to be existing where teachers

- could do their work in adequately equipped school buildings where the students among other things, have access to a school library or on-line services.

- have a salary comparable with other professions requiring the level of qualifications and responsibility, making it possible for them to live with dignity on the salary from their work and not to be forced to take a second or third job.

- have a right to receive a reasonable pension after retirement, which will make it possible for retired teachers to live with security and dignity.

The conference addressed the subject of Education Reform and passed a resolution which read in part, The Education International 2nd World Congress resolves to work for the resolution of an era of education as follows:

- All governments should guarantee public education as a right to every child.

- All governments should spend at least six per cent of their national budgets on education.

- All governments should build a system to enable children, who have dropped out of school, to return to school to resume their education at any time.

- All governments should improve school facilities to ensure efficient educational activities.

The subject of the protection of the rights of lesbian and gay education personnel was one of intense debate, following which the conference passed a resolution which highlighted a recommendation from Education International that:

- member organizations clearly state that discrimination on the basis of sexual orientation is a violation of human rights.

- member organizations support the right of teachers to choose whether or not to be open about their sexual orientation in the workplace.

Apart from the fore-mentioned resolutions, the following are some of the significant quotations extracted from presentations made by speakers addressing the Congress.

MARY FUTRELL – President of Education International

"Good teaching must be seen as a matter of life and death. Education must be seen as the need of children and not the greed of the nation. Teacher Trade Unions are not a barrier to economic progress, but a facilitator to economic progress."

"We do not need guns, we need books and computers for our children."

BOB CHASE – President, National Education Association of the U.S.A. (NEA)

"Regardless of where we live or what we believe, education is important."

BILL JORDAN – General Secretary, ICFTU

"At the head of our struggle is the elimination of child labour and poverty."

FRED VAN LEEUWEN – General Secretary, Education International

"To fight child labour, there needs to be more school and more teachers employed."

"Education International does not believe in Education Reform that slashes budgets."

"In low and middle income territories, many are leaving the profession because they can ill afford to stay in it economically."

FREDERICO MAYOR – Director-General, UNESCO

"Teachers built the fabric of democracy through the teaching of values, etc. They are instrumental in making children great citizens. Teachers in the classroom are working towards reducing the gender gap, knowledge gap and intolerance which leads to violence."

"It is not by computers that you will improve the quality of education, it has to be achieved through the awakening of people."

"Democracy is the key for sustainable education. Participation is essential for democracy . . . the teacher has to teach children how to think critically and how to live cooperatively."

"Without peace there is no education, justice nor freedom."

PRESIDENT OF THE UNITED STATES, BILL CLINTON

Speech delivered (in part) by the President of the United States of America to the 2nd World Congress of Education International, July 29, Washington, D.C.

"I believe in the global economy. Every nation should have international standards that meet international norms. We are working to reward the most innovative and successful teachers in our classrooms, to help those who fail to perform, or improve, and to encourage more of our best and brightest to enter the teaching profession, especially in the areas where there are a lot of school children in desperate need of more help . . .

"We are working to create better learning environments, by modernizing our schools and reducing class size, especially in the early grades, where research has shown that it may make positive and permanent difference in learning in our country . . .

"We are working hard to prepare our children for the demands of the information age, by connecting every classroom and library to the internet by the year 2000; and by training teachers in these new technologies . . .

"We are working to deal with one of America's most painful problems, the presence of violence in our schools. We have a zero tolerance for guns in our schools. Later this year, we will be having our first conference in Washington, on school safety. I hope and pray that this is not a problem in any country here represented, but if it is, we will be glad to have your ideas and to share ours with you. Teaching cannot succeed and learning cannot take place unless classrooms are safe, disciplined and drug free."

"In all my visits at home and abroad, I have found out that you can learn a lot about a country's future by visiting its public schools.

Does every child, rich or poor, have the same opportunity to learn? Are they engaged by patient, well-trained, and inspired teachers? Do they have access to materials they need to learn? Are they taught what they need to know to succeed in the country they will live in, and in the future, if they would create it?

Do they have opportunities to all the universities if they do well and deserve the chance to do so? Are the schools themselves safe, good places to learn?

We have to build a future together, if the answer to all these questions is 'yes', in every community and every nation. I believe we can build a future where every child, in every corner of the world, because of the explosion of technology and because of the dedication of teachers, will have the skill, the opportunity, the education to fulfil his or her God-given dream. I know this will happen if teachers lead the way".

In conclusion, congratulations are in order for Mrs. Marguerite Cummins-Williams, first vice-president of the Barbados Secondary Teachers' Union, who was re-elected to serve on the executive committee of Education International.

Members of the Barbados delegation to the Congress were Harry Husbands, President, B.U.T. (Delegate), Dennis de Peiza, B.U.T. (Observer), Marguerite Cummins-Williams and Joy Gittens – B.S.T.U. (Delegates).

Education International (E.I.) represents 23 million teachers worldwide.

> A Review of the 2nd World Congress of Education International
> Article published in the BUT's 'OUTLOOK MAGAZINE'

Societal Values Falling by the Wayside

The once proud Barbadian Society, noted for its acceptance and respect for law and order, and for its existence on strong traditional values, now seems to be a thing of the past.

Many have sought to advance what they perceive as sound reasons for this sad state of affairs. Initially, those who sought reasons for the negative trends that have emerged, placed the blame squarely on the failings of the educational system. As if destined to happen, teachers became the whipping horse of john public. Not even the Ministry of Education could resist the temptation of jumping on the bandwagon, to the point of even chastising teachers publicly.

In response to the public outcry, many changes have taken place within the education system. These have included the training and retraining of teachers to meet the new challenges associated with the demands of society and the era in which we live. The end result to all this is that little has changed. What has emerged is the fact that society on a whole has shown a reduced propensity to identify with the traditional values and norms.

The blatant disrespect shown for the police and church, two of the major institutions in society, clearly demonstrates the level to which our society has sunk. When one closely examines what underpins this change in the attitude to life amongst our youth and some adult members of the population, it is difficult to conceive who is to be blamed for the decline within the society. Could it be laid almost entirely at the feet of the educational system?

The negative forms of behaviour and attitude that now characterize the Barbadian landscape denote a drastic transformation of the expectations and outlook of a society, which prides itself on being grounded on an excellent education system that produces persons of high intellect. It is therefore a virtual mystery as to what has given rise to the degenerate behaviour which has taken root and threatens to undermine the stability of an orderly Christian society.

Whereas there has been the tendency in some quarters to levy the blame at doorsteps of some institutions for the downturn being experienced, the fact of the matter is that the society has allowed many unsavoury practices to become entrenched, without challenging them. In the desire to be identified as a liberalized society, no stone has been left unturned in the quest to transpose the North American culture in particular, into our own. Is it a case that in our attempt to liberalize our society that there has been a compromise on the standard of discipline to which we have grown accustomed?

The politicians have led the way by removing the death penalty for those under 18 years of age, who commit capital offences. The revised Education Act has imposed serious limitations on the exercising of corporal punishment in our schools. Teenage mothers now have the right to return to the classroom without reservation.

These are only but a few

of the privileges that our youth enjoy. While on the one hand it cannot be denied that these changes have come about as part of a progressive age, at the same time the drawback cannot be ignored. Who can turn a blind eye to the standard of dress now accepted in the church? What message does this send?

The old adage of spare the rod and spoil the child can easily be applied to the growing indiscipline that has taken over Barbados by storm. Take for example the problem with the school children on the ZR or Route Taxis and Minibuses. The unacceptable behaviour by the students who commute on these vehicles, and that of the drivers and conductors, has been known for some years now. This situation has been allowed to go unchecked, to the point that the police appear not to be effective in curbing the many forms of indisciplined behaviour associated with some users and operators.

It is unfortunate that in order to curb the behaviour and practices of the route taxis in particular, that Government has to resort to banning students in school uniforms from traveling in these vehicles. This problem is not unique to the route taxi, for the minibuses are equally as guilty. Therefore any ban should be applied across the board.

However, what is of immediate concern is how effective the measure to control the operations of these private sector vehicles would be. It is obvious that the youth not in school uniform would continue to ride these vehicles, if even it means changing from their uniforms into street clothes, as has been the practice. In short, instead of solving one problem, a monster may have been created.

The solution to the ZR and minibus problem seems rather simple, but it requires the political will, a form of draconian action, which would serve to drive into the heads of owners, drivers and conductors that disciplined operations must be the order of the day.

In order to show its might, Government ought to give consideration to the passage of legislation, which gives the police the right to impound any public service vehicle which is over-laden with passengers, or is found to be driven in a reckless manner on the roads of Barbados.

In both instances, the buses should be impounded for a minimum of 14 days, and driver and conductor have their licenses immediately suspended for a period of three months. If this fails to make a difference, then nothing will bring about corrective action.

Recognizing that all of those who practice misdeeds come out of our highly rated education system, it might not be true after all to state that the system is failing. Considering the intellectual powers that are utilized in the planning and execution of calculated unlawful acts, it must be said that these persons were well learnt.

It is therefore absolutely necessary for the society to adopt a get-tough approach, and to return to some of those measures that were followed in the past, in building an orderly Barbadian society.

There must also be sustained efforts to assist the schools in playing the role they ought to play. This could be achieved if parents seriously got down to carrying out their role as parents, and the Ministry of Education empowers and equips teachers to be more effective in their role of educating and training the nation's children.

The scourge of indiscipline that pervades the society is seemingly being encouraged and condoned by some members of the wider

Barbadian community.

The actions of most operators of route taxis and minibuses (drivers and conductors) are reprehensible. As reported, they practice dangerous driving practices, such as 'walking the dog and the milkshake'; all without due regard for their passengers, who are mainly school children. It is said that students now seek to enter into buses through the windows, rather than the doors. Other unsavoury practices in the vehicles are said to be encouraged.

This obvious indiscipline goes far beyond the school system. It is vital that all sectors of society pull their weight in order to curb this indiscipline. The work of the teachers in the school comes to naught, if the wider society does not make a conscious effort to support the training of our young people.

It seems the only way to safeguard the value and norms of the Barbadian society.

Dress Codes Ignored

It seemed like only yesterday that the Ministry of Education introduced regulatory measures, aimed at addressing the manner of dress of school children across the island. Although it can be said that there has been some general improvement in the standard of dress, the problem continues to exist. From observation, both boys and girls are equally guilty of exhibiting poor dress standards. The boys in the main were guilty of carrying themselves rather shabbily, often with their shirt tails flying, and pants falling below the waist line.

While the girls appear to be well attired, a closer look would suggest that their general appearance falls short of what is expected under the school rules. It is now commonplace to find girls dressed in short and close fitting uniforms. Lavish hairstyles, makeup and jewelry, compliment their outfits. Of late, jheri curl hairstyles and the wearing of braids, weave and wigs seem to have become part of the norm.

Dress fads among school children have been always with us, but it would seem that the young people of this current generation, have a more radical approach to dressing. As students move from the school to the tertiary level of education, the manner of dress can often be described as despicable. To some it would seem that to enter a tertiary institution is to receive a license to move one's manner of dress to the sublime.

In some instances, principals and teachers have a hard time in getting children to conform to school rules. Some students openly defy principals and teachers who attempt to correct their actions, and would go as far to refuse receiving corporal punishment at the hands of the Principal; gladly opting to be sent home instead.

In citing that the standard of dress in our schools has dropped, it is fair to say that this holds true for the wider Barbadian society. Many a reason has been advanced for this drastic change in behaviour. Without speculating, it can safely be argued, that there is a 'young at heart' wave that is permeating our society, and hence this apparently gives license to the fact that anything goes. In fighting this scourge, the responsibility is placed squarely on the shoulder of teachers to arrest the problem. In accepting the challenges, teachers generally by their mode of dress, set the example for their students to follow.

Adults, particularly parents and guardians, need to assume and discharge their responsibility in ensuring that high standards of discipline and deportment are maintained. Parents and guardians need to insist that their children or wards, leave for school properly dressed, and return home in like manner. There is the need for them to play their part, by insisting that the dress is in keeping with the school rules. Where parents, guardians and adults generally play an active role, most of the disciplinary problems in our schools, including dress, would be more quickly eliminated. Adults need to move away from seeming to support and encouraging indiscipline, where and whenever it raises its ugly head, and in whatever form. Adults therefore need to set the example.

Lets for a moment reflect on the manner of dress of many parents and guardians who are seen accompanying children to and from Primary School, or even those who come to Secondary Schools to have an audience with the Principal or teachers. Generally, the females seem to have lost all sense of decency and pride in themselves. It is more the norm than the exception to find them walking children to school, or loitering outside or on the school compound, with their bodies scantilly clothed.

The males are not to be left out, for they too are equally guilty. It is now normal to find bare back young men, usually attired in two or more pants, which are worn at various levels below the hip line, invading the privacy of schools.

Apart from having to cope with the problem of dress, the difficulties teachers face in attempting to promote a high level of discipline among school children, are exacerbated, considering the obscenity and vulgarity that is displayed by adults, both young and old alike. It would appear that some adults see nothing wrong with the current standard of dress or public conduct.

The challenge to curb the level of discipline and to remove those offensive traits, is fast becoming a daunting one. Teachers have the arduous task of trying to train and discipline students, who are being heavily influenced by the behavious and attitudes that are displayed by adults. In the meantime, serious damage is being done to our society.

Teachers in Barbadian schools ought to be credited by society for the sterling job they do. It is unfortunate that members of the profession are sometimes unfairly subjected to public ridicule, sometimes for acts not of their own making, or for a lapse on the part of an individual.

All apart, the profession continues to strive for excellence. It is reasonable to assume that teachers continue to understand and appreciate their role in the development of our people. Few can challenge the fact that teachers continue to set and maintain high standards. Teachers must be commended on their general conduct and deportment.

The commitment of teachers in working towards developing the minds of our nation's children is reflected through their continued thirst for knowledge, and in the efficient way in which they carry out their teaching assignments and civic responsibilities.

As teachers celebrate Education Month during this month of October, and Teachers Week, October 25 - 31, the public of Barbados needs to reaffirm its confidence in the teaching profession and give it all the support it deserves. Further, every young school leaver or university graduate who has an interest in entering the teaching profession, should proceed to do so, recognizing that it is a profession and not merely a vocation; and one which is a critical building process of our nation.

Persons desirous of entering the profession ought to realize that like any other profession, it has its pitfalls. However, accepting that teaching is a rather demanding and stressful job, which some may find not to be as financially rewarding as it ought to be, it nonetheless can be a rather gratifying experience.

Published: Daily Nation (Newspaper) Thursday October 29th, 1998, Page 5B; Headlined: 'Changing Trends, Falling Morals.'

Addressing Declining Values Amongst Our Youth

"Madam Principal, specially invited guests, Parents, guardians, well wishers, Graduands:

This evening I am particularly happy to be here, to share in this moment in time in the lives of these young ones, who form the 1998 graduating class of the Grant's Preparatory School.

Undoubtedly, this evening is a special one for them and I am sure that you parents, guardians and well wishers, are also pleased to share in the occasion.

Before I proceed further, I would ask the members of the graduating class to stand. I now invite you, the members of the audience, to recognize them by way of a special round of applause.

It is important at the outset to thank the Principal of the school, Ms. Denise Grant, for having invited me to deliver the keynote address at this graduation ceremony. When the invitation was initially extended, I offered neither a positive nor negative response. I allowed a few days to elapse as I quizzed my mind as to what I could say to a graduation class of 4-5 year olds. As I pondered, I knew that I could not disappoint my good friend Denise, since I doubted being able to ever erase the disappointment that she may have suffered.

In giving careful thought to the theme of this year's graduation, "Steps towards the future," I recognize that it provided me with the scope of directing the attention of parents, guardians, well-wishers, and indeed all adults assembled here, to their responsibility in moulding, shaping and influencing the lives of the young ones in our midst. I would want this evening, to focus your attention on the importance of the training we give our children, as we prepare and guide them through the stages of life.

As a teacher of over twenty years' experience, I have seen the drastic decline in the discipline, deportment, attitudes and performance of students. It should be evident to all conscious Barbadians that the moral fabric of the Barbadian society is no longer threatened, but is under severe attack.

All evidence points to the level of indecency and disrespect for law and order by both our youth and members of the adult population.

Our society is now the worst for all this, and so a rescue act is absolutely necessary, if some semblance of normalcy and respect for the value structure which formerly existed, is to be restored. It would seem to me that our policymakers do not have any immediate solutions to the problems we face. The role of such institutions as the church and school in the socialization process seems to be diminishing. The reasons for this are debatable. The church has seemingly lost its appeal. By this I mean there is an apparent movement away from the church in preference to other social and secular activities.

No longer are parents and guardians placing emphasis on sending or taking children to church and Sunday school as was the practice in the past. It is now more customary for young and old alike to gravitate to places where festive activities are to be found.

The role of the school has also been affected by the many changes in our society. I strongly believe that some of the fundamental changes to education in Barbados, as directed by our policymakers, have contributed to the existing state which characterizes our society.

Let us reflect together on what obtains in our schools to get a realistic picture of what I am attempting to put before you.

Have you stopped to consider how many of our schools still retain Religious Knowledge on their curriculum? It would be interesting to learn how many children of school age or those who have graduated from secondary school within the past decade can readily recite from memory, The Lord's Prayer, the Apostle's Creed, or even the Ten Commandments.

As the winds of change continue to blow, the discipline of students by way of corporal punishment has been removed from the hands of the rank and file teacher. Simply imagine the task of the teacher in trying to maintain a high level of discipline in an environment where students openly challenge and defy teachers, and who do not hesitate to remind teachers of restriction which the law imposes upon them. Added to this is the attitude displayed by some parents, which in itself is enough to frighten teachers into submission.

As we look towards the future - What hope do we see for our future generation of young people? Clearly if the current erosion of our norms and value system is allowed to continue, it is more than likely that the Barbadian society would challenge the United States, as far as the display of inept behaviour and violence is concerned.

Barbados can boast of having one of the best educational systems in the world, but this would mean nothing to this nation, if our children do not seize the opportunities provided. I therefore urge parents and guardians to see the importance of providing parental guidance. The training of our children must begin at home. Why should parents and guardians allow boys to come to school wearing earrings in their ears, scarves on their heads and pants below the waist? Why should girls be allowed to come to school as if they are going to a party or preparing for a beauty contest? Why should a blind eye be paid to their seductive mode of dress?

It seems to me that adults contribute in no small measure to the poor standards in this society. Our young people tend to follow the examples set by adults, and so the obvious silence of many adults virtually gives licence to the behaviour that the youth exhibit.

Let us take a moment to examine some of the things for which our adults are directly responsible. Take for example how some parents dress young boys and girls. Toddlers are dressed in the latest outfits and often laden with jewelry. Mothers and daughters go out dressed as partners and sometimes appear to be in competition with each other. Often the level of exposure of the body is appalling.

I say all this to point out that adults need to begin again to set the example, if, as we look towards the future, there is to be a change in the general attitude and outlook of our people.

I put it to you that we have already lost two generations of our youth. Many young people between the ages of 15-25 are already parents, and some between 30-35 are grandparents. Our society should be concerned with the lifestyles of persons between 15-35 and the level of parental guidance they are offering to their offspring.

It is important that Barbadians halt the shift toward an American identity, and follow the accepted patterns our culture promotes.

It is to be noted that this society attempted to follow the American system by removing corporal punishment in a direct way from the classroom. Today, violence has overtaken American schools, and by extension the wider American society.

The severity of disciplinary problems in American schools has led to loud calls for the reintroduction of corporal punishment in schools.

Let us, in looking toward the future, attempt to avoid the pitfalls of the American educational system, if only for the good of our young ones, who will be the men and women of tomorrow. Let me briefly cite two news items coming out of the U.S.A., on which I urge you to ponder.

Firstly, CNN Morning edition of Friday, June 19, 1998, reported that a study showed that approximately one million children in schools across America were carrying guns to school, and of that number, two- thirds admitted to using drugs.

Secondly, the Thursday June 18, 1998 edition of THE LOCAL DAILY NATION Newspaper reported that a teacher was fired for praying with a class. You can draw your own conclusions of the messages which these two stories convey to us. If we are serious about ensuring that our educational system does not fail our children, then I strongly urge that we speak out against any changes in education which will not serve their best interests.

I challenge you this evening, without reservation, to follow the teachings as set out in Proverbs 22:6, "Train up a child in the way he should go, and when he is old, he will not depart from it."

And to you children, I want you to learn and follow the Fifth Commandment, which teaches you to be obedient. It goes like this "Honor your father and mother, that your days may be long in the land, which the Lord thy God giveth thee."

I thank you, ladies and gentlemen, for your attention. Finally, I extend best wishes and continued prosperity to the Grant's Preparatory School."

Keynote Address At The Graduation Ceremony Of The Grants's Preparatory School At The Duncan Moore Education Centre , Sharon, St. Thomas, Thursday July 9th, 1998

Remarks to ILO Workshop on Occupational Safety and Health in Construction

First, let me commend the Ministry of Labour and Social Security for having taken the decision to organize this workshop on Occupational Safety and Health in Construction. The Labour Department is also to be complimented for its role in organizing the event.

The Congress of Trade Unions and Staff Associations of Barbados on whose behalf I speak, lauds the Ministry and by extension the Labour Department for the efforts made in seeking to put in place policy documents to deal with two of the most hazardous sectors, in those of agriculture and construction.

Last year the Ministry of Labour & Social Security and the Labour Department in conjunction with the International Labour Organization, held a similar workshop on the subject of agriculture. Since staging the workshop, the Labour Department has been working towards the writing of a policy on occupational safety and health in agriculture.

The fact that today's effort is directed at developing a policy in safety and health in construction, clearly demonstrates the commitment of the Labour Department in working towards developing a health and safety culture in Barbados.

When we consider the number of persons employed in the construction sector, particularly so at a time when the island is experiencing a building boom, this focus on occupational safety and health is timely.

CTUSAB recognizes that the current programme results from the foresight of the Labour Department, the work of the National Advisory Commission on Occupational Safety and Health, whose mission is to advise the Ministry on health and safety issues.

The labour movement is aware of the fact that the ILO recognizes construction along with mining, agriculture and forestry as among the most hazardous industries in the world. Mindful of the hazards of the construction industry, the Barbados Workers' Union, which remains as the single private sector trade union on the island, has over the past fifty years, worked relentlessly in attempting to establish a safety culture in construction.

Records of the negotiated collective agreements between the BWU and unionized construction companies would show that from as early as the 1960's, the union was visionary in its approach to safety and health in the sector. It sought to move companies beyond providing basic personal protective equipment, such as gloves and goggles, to making provision for medical check ups, and for safety and health training.

It is important that the growing global concern of accidents recorded in the construction industry does not escape our attention; although it may be argued that the casualty rate in Barbados is not significant enough to cause for any alarm at this time. Having recently reviewed some accidents statistics in the construction sector for the period 1999 - 2002, as sourced from the Labour Department, my findings revealed that an increase was recorded.

If we were to take a global view of the situation, the ILO Report for the World Day for Safety and Health at Work 2005, highlighted the fact that every year 60,000 fatal accidents are recorded in the construction industry around the world, with one fatal accident occuring every ten (10) minutes. That report also indicated that the construction industry is associated with a high number of job related accidents and diseases. The findings of the report speak to the fact that 30% of construction workers suffer from back pains and other musculoskeletal disorders.

This to my mind highlights the need for a premium to be placed on safety training as one way to reduce both injuries and fatalities. I must therefore stress the point that productivity must not be placed before safety.

In Barbados, the experience is that the most serious injuries and fatalities are recorded in the informal sector. As you would recall, the most recent occurred when two men lost their lives, after repeatedly inhaling toxins in a well which they were cleaning.

The labour movement is primarily concerned with the operations of the informal sector and foreign based companies that operate in Barbados. In Barbados, small companies are primarily engaged as subcontractors. These companies for the most part do not have the financial resources to invest in equipment or training for workers. In treating to this, it is important that the factory inspectorate becomes far more vigilant in this area.

With respect to foreign based companies, the labour movement is concerned that these companies bring their nationals to the island to work on projects. These workers are not unionized. The movement takes issue with the fact that it is unaware of the conditions under which workers operate. We are not privy to the wages that they are paid, or other specific conditions of employment.

Finally, I urge employers to see it not only as their responsibility to put basic safety measures in place, but to recognise that they have an added responsibility to ensure that employees comply with safety rules and standards.

I wish to thank the Ministry of Labour and Social Security for having invited CTUSAB to participate in this workshop. I can assure you that you can look forward to more food for thought, when my colleague, Orlando 'Gabby' Scott addresses you later in the proceedings, on the subject of CTUSAB's perspective on 'The status of Safety and Health in the Construction Industry.

Violence in Schools What Can Be Done to Protect Teachers?

The topical subject of 'violence in schools' is almost certain to engage the attention of any gathering of teacher trade unionist in any part of the world. This subject is expected to be high on the agenda when delegates from Sixteen Caribbean Islands, assemble in Barbados for the 29th Biennial Conference of the Caribbean Union of Teachers, at Divi South Winds Hotel, August, 1999.

The scourge of violence has touched almost every one of the member units of the C.U.T., and there seems to be no immediate solutions at hand in addressing this looming problem.

The trail of tragedy which has plagued the school system in the United States of America, cannot and should not be ignored here in the Caribbean region, and particularly so in Barbados. Back in the 1980's, a fatal stabbing was recorded at the Foundation School. Since then there have been numerous cases of physical assault on both students and teachers, in which weapons of one sort or another were used.

Recent reports of students being involved in alleged bomb-making activity at two St. Michael educational institutions, is extremely disturbing. On the heels of the Columbine High School massacre in the United States, Caribbean teachers must become increasingly aware that it can happen here.

The burning question now is: What can be done to protect teachers? The answer to this and other related questions should be at the centre of discussion at the one-week 29th Biennial Conference of the C.U.T. August 8-14.

The teachers of the region ought to seize this opportunity to assess reasons for the emerging trend of violence in our schools. They would be challenged to analyze the theories put forward by the experts that this pattern of behaviour is linked to the phenomena of gang presence and activity, hate motivated behaviour and drugs.

The acute nature of school violence in the United States of America has captured the interest of educators there. It became a major point of discussion at the 1999 Representative Assembly of the National Education Association of the United States of America (NEA), which was held in Orlando, Florida, June 29-July 6.

The Orlando Sentinel of July 3, quoted the following statement made by Mr. Bob Chase, the re-elected president of the NEA.:

"School violence is a complex beast, we must not be paralyzed by it."

In identifying the root cause of violence in school, the paper also quoted President Chase as having stated, "part of the problem is that we live in a society that glamorizes and mass-markets violence."

Whatever may be the root cause(s) of the problem of school violence, what now is important is how to stem the tide of this anti-social behaviour. One way of tacking the problem was advanced by U.S. Rep. Patrick Kennedy in addressing members of the NEA.

According to the Orlando Sentinel, July 3: "Kennedy drew rousing applause when he said teachers should have the right to firmly discipline children and remove trouble makers from the classroom."

This comment holds immense interest for Barbadian Schools. What holds equal interest, is the response of a teacher to Kennedy's comment that was also published by the Orlando Sentinel.

The paper cited that "one teacher in the audience stood up and emphasized that principals often do not back teachers in such instances because they are "paranoid" about possible lawsuits by parents."

Looking objectively at the situation, the Caribbean Union of Teachers has a responsibility to continue to focus on promoting non-violence in schools. The regional body must consider strategies that could help to bring about an environment at schools, where teachers and students should feel safe from physical, verbal and psychological violence.

It should come as no surprise if the Caribbean Union of Teachers were to endorse the strategy of the NEA which promotes the equation, safe schools = safe communities + safe families.

This equation promotes the view that schools are not inherently unsafe, but if schools are to be safe places, then safety in communities and families must be addressed.

Tribute to John Henry Cumberbatch

Senator Cynthia Forde, Senator Leroy Trotman, members of the Executive Committee, past presidents and general secretaries of the B.U.T., distinguished guests, members of the Cumberbatch family, colleagues, ladies and gentlemen.

This evening we have gathered here at our "Merryhill" headquarters, to pay tribute to the memory of the late John Henry Cumberbatch.

Your presence here on this occasion, is in itself a fitting way of paying tribute to one who is worthy of the highest acclaim, we in the Barbados Union of Teachers can offer.

For the greater part of 23 years, John Cumberbatch virtually made this 'Merryhill' headquarters his home. We could not have chosen a more appropriate place to assemble to pay tribute to his memory.

Our memorial this evening has taken a somewhat different form from that to which we are accustomed. This I can assure you is in keeping with family wishes, who would want us to identify with John, in a manner consistent with his philosophy.

Let me at this point recognize the presence of John's immediate relatives who are here with us this evening. We the members of the B.U.T. family would want you to know that we share in your loss at this time.

It is often said that it is not until the passing of an individual, that tribute is paid to the work and accomplishments of that person. More often than not, this holds true. However, I am pleased to say that the B.U.T. has not found itself wanting in this respect, as it was the practice to honour the name of John Cumberbatch whenever the opportunity presented itself. Nothing would have pleased this organization more than to have had the pleasure of fittingly honouring John during his lifetime as we are doing this evening, had he permitted us to do so.

John Cumberbatch was not one for ceremonies or accolades. We could well imagine the look on his face if he were physically present to witness these proceedings, being held in his honour.

Notwithstanding this, we consider it our bounding duty to honour the memory of John Henry Cumberbatch, who beyond a shadow of a doubt was one of the great Barbadian and Caribbean Trade Union leaders of this century.

John Cumberbatch was born on July 23rd, 1940 into what may be described as a middle class home. He was known for his exceptional intellectual ability.

He was a multi-talented individual, but most of all he demonstrated a love for journalism.

In developing his journalistic skills, he worked with the Gleaner newspaper in Jamaica and the Advocate News here in Barbados. In his chosen profession of teaching, he gave 23 years of service, during which time he worked at the Parkinson Memorial School.

John brought his journalistic skills to bear in the B.U.T., and was instrumental in getting the B.U.T. OUTLOOK Magazine on the road. It is significant to note that he maintained his ties with the OUTLOOK Magazine to the end.

Outside of all other things, the B.U.T. held a special place in the heart of John Cumberbatch. He was committed to building and developing a vibrant organization, which would focus on bringing about fundamental changes to the educational system, to the betterment of the system and the teaching profession on the whole. His association with the union dates back to 1965 when it was then a division of the Civil Service Association.

The death of John on Monday, April 21, 1997, removed his physical presence from the Barbados Union of Teachers, but what it did not do was to remove from history's pages, the record of his work to the cause of the local and regional labour movement.

In the years ahead and maybe even now, some will wonder as to who John Cumberbatch was and what he meant to B.U.T. History will record that he was the chief architect of B.U.T's independence as a trade union, and became its first president in 1974. Most importantly, his dynamism, stamina, hard work and vision laid the bedrock for the B.U.T's growth as a vibrant and respected body.

John's association with the B.U.T. was accurately summarized in the 21st edition of the Outlook Magazine. As stated, "John's life was B.U.T., he gave of his blood, sweat and tears to nurture this organization during those early years. Of course there were others walking and working with him [this refers to persons such as Carl Springer, Alfred Trotman and the like], but none so carried the burden of feeling the energy of the young organization".

He accepted the challenge of leadership and carried it manfully. Stanley Mayers, who served with him as General Secretary during the period 1977-1979 in describing Cumberbatch, stated, "As a union leader he was absolutely fearless, when doing teacher business he feared no one, from Prime Ministers down."

As a leader, he achieved much for the B.U.T. He developed a new thrust toward industrial relations and professional development. He successfully led the struggle for better salaries and conditions of employment for teachers. His dynamic leadership brought a new lease of life to the profession.

John was known for his influential and inspirational leadership. No better assessment could have been made of his leadership than that voiced by Stanley Mayers. According to Mayers, "He was an inspiration; he dared us to be different. He dared us to stand up for our rights. The true measure of his achievement as a union teacher laid in his ability to inspire members to give their talents to the union."

There can be no doubt whatsoever that John inspired members to give of their talents to the union. The record of his influence on his colleagues at the Parkinson Memorial School speaks for itself.

As you would have learnt the brainstorming for a plan of action leading to an independent B.U.T. started at Parkinson Memorial School. John's influence could be said to have contributed to the fact that many of his colleagues at the school, joined him in the struggle, to the extent that the school has a tradition of producing many who serve this organization at the highest level.

John was a hard worker who engaged himself in the struggle to bring about meaningful change within the educational system. His calling was not motivated by self interest, nor propelled by the desire for material gain or recognition.

He was revolutionary in intent, for his aim was to affect a complete overhaul of the educational system. He viewed that such an overhaul would promote greater equality within the system, thus eliminating the status quo where some benefited more than others. In short, he envisaged a complete overhaul of the system so that Harrison College [his alma mater] which for so long was residing in the heart of the ghetto, but being the node of the system, would become integrated into the ghetto.

John left no doubt about his radical outlook. He was reported to have said: "As far back as 1971 my ideas on the education system were so radical that I doubted I would have received support from those who were involved in the union struggle with me."

He centered his struggle around the Common Entrance Examination. Consistent with his view that there should be equality within the educational system, he argued that there should be no Common Entrance Examination and that pupils should move automatically from primary to secondary school.

John Cumberbatch died without realizing this dream. The pitfalls of the Common Entrance Examinations continue to be the subject of debate, since the changes effected seem not to have made any fundamental difference to what has existed for time immemorial. He has therefore left us the task to continue the struggle to remove what can only be described as an impediment which has plagued the system.

If there is one way we can seek to preserve the memory of John Cumberbatch, it is to associate ourselves with his philosophy that there is no place for hypocrisy. Nothing troubled him more than to see policies and practices which were instituted and followed, which ran contrary to what the system intended to achieve.

Added to this we can complement the foundation he has laid, by following his lead in dealing vigorously with issues which confront us without fear or favour; never losing sight of our focus in the process.

Those who carry on the baton of leadership within the B.U.T. must recognize that our founding father John Cumberbatch engineered the birth of the B.U.T. to fight against the shortcomings of the educational system, and therefore we must commit ourselves to preserve our gains and to continue the fight towards a continuous improvement of the system.

As a final tribute to John let us recognize his commitment to the cause of the teaching profession, for it was his desire to influence change throughout the Caribbean which led him to the regional scene. As president of the Caribbean Union of Teachers he wasted no time in making his presence felt.

John, as a good teacher, left us one lesson, simply put: 'Live in accordance with your philosophy of life.' This embraces being true to oneself, for as a well known saying goes, 'how can you be true to someone else if you can't be true to yourself'.

In remembering him, let us forever focus on the tremendous part he played in the life of this organization, and not on whom he was or what one expected him to be.

Many of us would remember John for his association with the Rastafarian movement, with which he publicly identified on resigning from the teaching profession in 1979. This was part of the radical nature of John, but in doing so, he was true to himself. Now that he has departed this life, let us do as he would admonish us, and follow the words of the legendary Bob Marley: "Get up, stand up, stand up for your rights . . . but don't give up the fight."

As we come to the end of these formal tributes, let me assure you that the Executive Committee is cognizant of the need to give serious consideration towards identifying a means of keeping the memory of John alive.

Let me take this opportunity to thank all who have contributed to this evening of tribute. Your support and participation is appreciated.

May John eternally rest in peace.

> Speech made on the occasion of 'The Tribute To John Cumberbatch' B.U.T Headquarters, 9th May, 1997;
> Dennis de Peiza, President, Barbados Union of Teachers.

Lengthening of the School Year

Over the past three years, the proposed changes within the realm of education and the teaching profession in particular, have been countless. The rationale and significance of some of these changes remain unexplained. To go further, the basis on which some of these changes were grounded, seemed to lack depth, and hence can hardly be justified.

Such seems to be the case regarding the issue of the lengthening of the school year.

The point must be established and accepted that change is inevitable. Change however should not be meaningless. Whenever it is the intention to effect change, there should be clear justification for such.

In an age in which major policy changes are made based on some sound documented research, or on indicators which emerge from some empirical data or statistical analysis, one would come to expect that the data collected through the scientific mode of study, would in fact inform the decision-making process in education.

If per chance there is such data available, which serves to inform the thinking of personnel within the Ministry of Education, then the latter has a responsibility to share it first with the teachers' unions and the public thereafter.

As the debate continues, no information has come to the fore to suggest that the teachers, who are the professionals in the delivery of education, see the need for a change to the current length of the school day. It is only reasonable, fair and just, that those who are directly involved in the system and who will be affected by any change to it, be given a realistic opportunity to have an input. The point must be clearly made that a fundamental decision such as this one, cannot be made on impulse, or on the basis of a judgement call.

In attempting to identify reason(s) for the suggested change, the only possible one that surfaces is the contention that teachers benefit from more vacation leave than the average public servants do. It would be amazing if this was the only rationale being used. Taking into consideration the stress that has been placed on the notion of productivity as of late, one may be led to conclude that this has a direct bearing on the current wave of thinking. If this is at all so, it would be extremely distressing if the inference is made that there is a fall off in the productivity of teachers, both inside and outside of the classroom.

The demands placed on teachers are already excessive. Outside of the formal classroom setting, most teachers are involved in extra curricular activities. This extends to work in the community in various forms. Teachers receive no additional pay for their involvement in these activities and do so at much personal sacrifice. It ought to be recognized that the time spent, amounts to be part of the man-hours, in the working life of the teacher. It is therefore unreasonable to demand more of the teacher, whose workload extends beyond the classroom. Outside of the classroom the teacher ultimately interacts with children and adults in a formal or informal education process.

Parents, guardians and members of the Barbadian community at large are not oblivious to the amount of work that teachers do and the sacrifices that they are called upon to make in meeting their professional obligations, and being of service to the community.

It is worth the while to reflect on the hours teachers spend in preparing students for cultural and sporting events after school. This would include events such as NIFCA and the Crop Over Festival. The time spent in accompanying students to such activities, must also be brought into the equation.

Mention also has to be made of the summer camps and the various overseas educational tours that are arranged. What can be said of those teachers who are involved in sports? They are called to work long hours after the end of the school day and even on Saturdays, Sundays and public holidays. At the end of the day, the fact remains that most teachers who are involved, get no additional remuneration, far less recognition of any kind.

The idea to lengthen the school year should not be allowed to gain currency. Teachers are already overworked and underpaid. If the authorities pursue this idea, then they have to come to grips with the principle that increase in work means increase in pay. Further, it cannot be ignored, that any change to the school year would mean a fundamental change to the conditions of the service of teachers.

The suggestion that there should be a change to the length of the school day is basically the same as that promoted some years ago by the then Minister of Education, the Honourable Billie Miller. The Minister at that time sought in effect to lengthen the hours of work of teachers by proposing that there should be school on Saturdays. This was dismissed with the greatest contempt, but it would seem that the idea has now been resurrected, only that it is being advocated in a different form.

It is difficult to conceptualise what has given rise to the initiation of a campaign for a change to the length of the school year. Whatever is the reason, the stance taken by the teachers' unions to resist any such change, above all things, is what matters. There is nothing to suggest that there is merit in effecting such a change, or that it is a matter of any priority, as far as enhancing the delivery of education is concerned.

This subject is sure to stimulate healthy debate in education circles. It could arouse wider public interest, depending upon the thrust that is given to the debate. Considering that they are more pressing issues in education which need to be addressed, maybe the current focus is misdirected. Our education system would be better served, if educators and policy makers were to focus on finding meaningful solutions to the many problems in our schools. Much time and energy should be spent in attempting to put into effect, better terms and conditions for the employment of teachers.

From a teacher's perspective, there can be little support for the lengthening of the school year. It would be a blessing if teachers were to learn that such a change, though not preferred, would solve the problems of indiscipline, drugs and violence in schools, resolve the inadequacy of teaching materials, equipment and facilities, conquer the pitfalls of the administration of our schools, in addition to resolving the many other difficulties teachers face in carrying out their duties on a daily basis.

There can be no mistaking the fact that the Education Act empowers the Minister to make a change to the length of the school day. Further no one should play ignorant to where the bastion of legislative powers lies.

Published: Weekend Nation Newspaper, Friday, June 18th, 1998
Headlined: "Lengthening The School Year"

Sports Versus Academics

Any suggestion that there is much down-time lost to sports in our schools needs to be justified by the proponents of such a view. It is inconceivable that in this phase of our educational development that principals, teachers and educational administrators, including policy makers, could share such a view.

If we are talking about the total development of our children, it would be interesting to learn the basis for the suggestion that the time spent by our students in the preparation and participation of organized sports events, erodes teaching time.

This type of thinking reflects that there remains a heavy academic bias in our schools system. It goes further to suggest that there is little importance attached to the teaching of Physical Education and the development of sports in our schools.

Education Psychologists have stressed the importance attached to the all-round development of children. Teachers passing through Erdiston College would have learnt of the importance of developing the cognitive, psychomotor and affective domain of children. Given this, it must be understood that the development of these domains are facilitated through teaching or coaching, and in the actual participation in sporting activities. Sports should not be down-played in school, since they contribute to the physical and psychological development of the child.

If we are to accept that the much contact time in schools is lost to sporting activities, then it leaves us to reason that the school would be failing those students who have sporting talents and abilities and a desire to develop them. Further, to do so would be to give support to a system which by practice hinders the overall development of students.

To classify time dedicated to sports as lost time, represents an ignorance of the role sports play in the life of a school. The successes which a school records does much to boost the image of the institution. Most importantly, it serves to motivate the student body in other areas of school life.

For the individual student, particularly those who may not be academically inclined, success however limited, brings with it a sense of achievement. This helps to boost self-esteem and provides for some form of recognition. In an educational system where the failure rates are high, there is ample evidence to support the fact that many students are unable to handle the basics. It is the responsibility of the school to provide opportunities to develop the skills, abilities and talents of students in sports, or in other disciplines on the curriculum.

If we are to continue to measure the success of students graduating from school based simply on the number of C.X.C Examinations passed, then it could be argued that this measurement is biased, since it does not take into consideration the achievements of students for which there is no form of certification.

However, it is interesting to note that many of our academic and non-academic school leavers who were heavily involved in sports, have gone on to excel at the local, regional and international level. Had the school not provided them with the opportunity through the Physical Education programme, there was the distinct possibility that their rate of development would have been hindered.

It makes sense, to pay greater attention to the development of the sporting programme in our schools, rather than to seek to reduce its significance, based on a false premise that to play sports is to make sport.

It should be obvious that sports is big business, with sportsmen being some of the best paid people in the world. Let's recognize that the school is a place for developing abilities and talents. If there is a consciousness of this, then greater resources should be made available in schools to enhance the quality of the offering in the Sports Programme. These should include manpower resources, equipment and facilities. There should also be recognition of the need for more avenues for training of Physical Education teachers.

If the contention is that the down-time lost to sports is based on the fact that the basic infrastructure is lacking and that class sizes should be reduced to make them more meaningful and productive, then the claim may be modestly justified. However, it is unreasonable to classify the time spent on sports in our schools as down-time lost since the system continues to produce quality athletes in many disciplines.

The fact that the demand for athletic scholarships has grown and that students from sporting backgrounds now compete for the award of a Barbados Scholarship, justifies how important it is to allocate time to sporting activities in our schools.

It should not be necessary to remind persons that a healthy body leads to a healthy mind. Participating in sporting activities will surely lead to development of a healthy body.

Chapter Four

Health

The Health Status of the Work Force

The aging factor of the Barbadian workforce cannot be ignored as a single phenomenon which has the potential of reducing levels of productivity. The reduction in productivity levels may also be linked to the declining health of able bodied members of the workforce.

What then are these contributing factors that currently impact on the declining health of our workforce?

We start by examining those associated with the workplace. Workplace stress, poor workplace health environments, occupational diseases, such as carpel tunnel syndrome, and failure to observe workplace safety and health practices, are among those that readily come to mind.

Considering the lifestyles followed by individuals the magnitude of the problem is amplified. The lack of exercise resulting in obesity, generally poor diets, smoking and the excessive use of alcohol, are among those identified by the health experts. It would seem logical that in an effort to preserve our workforce, increasing emphasis needs to be placed on wellness educational programmes that create a greater awareness amongst the workforce community.

In developing a medium through which matters of this nature ought to be addressed, it makes good sense to encourage the promoting of workplace safety and health committees. This provides an excellent opportunity for employers and employees to work together, as they seek to address a common interest: that of the welfare of the human resource.

Current local employment statistics show that more women are now employed than men. Added to this, single-parent homes in which the female is the sole bread winner, is now a prominent feature in our society. The high incidence of breast and cervical cancer, diabetes, hypertension and heart disease among women, places upon them a responsibility to pay more attention to their health.

Equally so, this applies to men who are plagued by prostate cancer, hypertension and heart disease. What is interesting in relation to women, are the findings of a recent study of the World Health Organization. That study revealed that heart disease is now killing significantly more women than men. It is estimated that 8.6 million world wide died of the disease, as compared to 7.9 million men.

According to Catherine Le Gables Camus, Assistant Director General, Non Communicable Diseases of the World Health Organization, the study revealed that "Although most women fear cancer, particularly breast cancer, they do not make the same efforts to safeguard themselves from heart disease, which is eminently preventable."

The study also highlighted the fact that a woman is about eighteen times more likely to die of heart disease than breast cancer. Furthermore, that a women is more likely to have a stroke than a man.

What does this say to our labour force? It strongly suggests that we need to eat better and exercise more. What it also says is that our workplaces need to be less stressful. If employers are to truly reflect that they care about their employees, then they must provide for them, health insurance schemes, offer smoke and hazard free workplace environments, as well as health and fitness individuals or family group packages.

Such incentive programmes are normally found within private sector organizations. It is about time that Government, as the largest single employer, begins to demonstrate its fullest commitment to promoting the safety and health of its employees by offering suitable incentive group packages. Public Sector Unions should seek to negotiate provisions associated with any such packages, Government is urged to give careful examination to any such initiative.

CTUSAB has already made an approach to Government with regard to exploring the possible implementation of a group Medicare Scheme, which would serve to provide coverage for all public servants. It is important that the Social Partners work together in developing programmes to safeguard the health of this nation's workforce, in an effort to stimulate greater productivity and to enhance job satisfaction.

Unpublished Article

Occupational Safety and Health

I welcome the opportunity this morning to participate in this the official launch of Occupational Safety and Health Week 2003.

Right across the globe, the issue of Occupational Safety and Health has emerged as a major workplace agenda item that has captured the attention of employers, employees, governments, trade unions and international bodies such as the International Labour Organization.

I contend that the importance attached to this issue emerges out of a growing recognition of the value of labour. Inasmuch as I regret to say it, the value attached to labour may be, in some quarters, tied only to profits to be realized at the end of the financial year.

In the main, there is tremendous concern over the down-time or loss of man hours being experienced in the workplace, where employees are being forced off the job as a consequence of work-related illnesses and accidents. On the other hand, there is growing concern over the diminishing state of health of able-bodied workers, whose health is being compromised by the lack of a strong safety and health culture being developed in the workplace.

I have carefully noted the chosen theme for this week of 'Workplace Safety and Health – Supporting Productivity'.

In the context of the growing fall-out being experienced in the local employment sectors, where workplace-related accidents and illnesses have impacted on productivity, the theme for the week is more than appropriate.

Mr. Anthony Sobers, Chief Economist of the Barbados National Productivity Council, captures the magnitude of the problem in his paper of July 2001, entitled: 'The Growth of on the job injuries in Barbados. The Impact on Organizational Performance.'

In that paper he wrote: "The Barbados experience of on the job injuries has not been encouraging. Presently, seven per cent (7%) of our workforce becomes injured on the job or 7 228 persons out of a workforce of 117 110 persons have become injured on the job".

Referring to the period 1993-2000 he noted that each case averages 20 days sick leave. "The average time lost from injuries has increased by 81 per cent over the said period. In fact, the country has lost 4.3 per cent of its output due to injuries on the job alone."

He went on to underscore the point that the situation had reached a critical stage, given the rapid increase in the number of reported injuries. Statistical data for the year 2002 confirmed that the severity of the injuries has been increasing from 16 to 29 days per case.

This analysis paints a gloomy picture as far as a down-turn in productivity is concerned within the Barbadian employment sector.

Considering the fact that the negative fall-out is not limited to the enterprise level, but goes further to severely impact on the Gross Domestic Product, this should become a matter of immense concern to all interests within the labour sector.

This point is accentuated when we examine global trends. Recent information put out by the ILO in a document captioned: 'Facts on safe work', estimates that four (4%) per cent of the world's GDP is lost due to accidents at work and work-related diseases.

What is even more important is the fact the ILO records that each year approximately two million women and men die as a result of occupational accidents and work-related diseases.

Against this backdrop, it becomes imperative that a strong safety and health culture is developed within the workplace, for such would be beneficial to workers, employers, Governments and trade unions.

It is therefore the responsibility of every employer to ensure that as far as it is practicable, that the safety and health of workers is not compromised.

Further, it stands to reason that the creation and sustaining of a safe and healthy work place environment must be seen as paramount, if a high degree of quality and productivity is to be realized.

If we accept that the matter of improved safety and health at work is paramount, then there is every good reason for a sense of collective responsibility to be demonstrated, which reflects itself in a coordinated effort by the Government, the unions and the workers themselves.

In working towards promoting best workplace safety and health practices, Government should be urged to give active consideration to adopting ILO Occupational Safety and Health Convention No. 155. To do so, would be to promote the implementation of a set of standards that support a safety and health culture at work.

As we move to effect meaningful change, now may be the appropriate time to lobby for the introduction of legislation that mandates that Safety and Health Committees be established in all workplaces.

In addition to this, there should be the creation by the state of an adequate inspection mechanism and the imposition of sanctions against employers who do not comply with their obligations. As we focus on how to reduce safety and health risks and to promote productivity, I strongly suggest that attention is focused on the five key elements of Policy, Training, Procedures, Measurement and Enforcement.

- With respect to policy, the management ought to set forth the will and direction of the organization.

- Training must be focused on determining and validating the competencies of workers in relation to hazards.

- As far as procedures are concerned, there is the need to establish and provide written procedures for jobs which have the potential to cause or create a serious injury.

- Measurement must form part of the process, as it is absolutely necessary that systems be put in place to evaluate training procedures and programmes, as a means of accessing their adequacy.

- Enforcement is to be seen as all-important, as this is the only sure means of ensuring compliance to the company's rules and procedures.

Let me at the risk of being repetitive, and for what it is worth, seek to reinforce in the minds of employers and employees, that productivity is tied to good work ethics, but equally so, it is also tied to a culture that promotes the interest of the safety and health of all who occupy or frequent the workplace.

With your permission, permit me to publicly commend Mr. Orlando 'Gabby' Scott of the Barbados Workers Union, on the excellent work that he has done and continues to do, as an advocate in promoting safety and health in the workplace.

In closing, I seek to re-affirm CTUSAB's commitment as a member of the Social Partnership, in promoting workplace safety and health, as expressed in Section 5.11 of Protocol Four, which speaks to adopting a meaningful tripartite approach to confront the new and varied occupational safety and health challenges that affect the workplace.

It is now left for me to wish for a successful week, out of which I hope would emerge meaningful ideas and suggestions that would help to address workplace occupational safety and health issues, as a means towards enhancing productivity.

Thank you ladies and gentlemen for your attentiveness. I am obliged to you Mr. Chairman.

Dennis de Peiza, General Secretary, Congress of Trade Unions and Staff Associations of Barbados, 2003

Prevention of Alcoholism and Drug Dependency

Following upon the national debate on the subject of the introduction and legalizing of Breathalyzer testing in Barbados, today's exercise can be considered as part of the ongoing effort to raise the national consciousness of our people about the negative impact which alcoholism has and continues to inflict on the Barbadian society.

The introduction of Breathalyzer testing in the metropolitan cities has had its genesis in the need to find a meaningful strategy that is aimed at reducing the high incidence of road deaths. It is therefore reasonable to conclude that the increasing number of serious vehicular accidents on our roads in Barbados that result either with serious injuries and/or death, is enough to have generated calls for Breathalyzer testing to be considered as an option in addressing the escalating problem.

It is clear that the loss of life and/or serious injury means a loss of an able-bodied person from the workforce and hence contributes to a down-turn in productivity. The added consequence is the strain that all this imposes on the nation's social services.

The experts view that bad driving habits and the fact that many persons have been found to be driving under the influence of alcohol, contribute significantly to the carnage on our roads.

There is a growing sense that alcohol is now being readily consumed by young and old alike, and by both sexes. It is against this backdrop that it becomes necessary to identify a set of meaningful strategies that are specifically focused at making operators of vehicles far more responsible when using the roads of Barbados. The bottom line is the protection of vehicle operators, passengers and pedestrians alike.

CTUSAB recognizes that the roadways and byways formed the workplaces of many of this nation's employees. The lives, safety and health of these individuals are daily placed at risk as they travel across the length and breadth of this land in executing their duties. Mindful of this, the Congress commits itself to working with all relevant agencies through the medium of educational fora, in calling workers' attention to their responsibility when using the roadways of Barbados on a daily basis.

Whereas CTUSAB does not have a policy position on the matter of legalizing Breathalyzer testing in Barbados, it is however conscious of the fact that some appropriate action must be considered, if operators of vehicles are to be guided towards developing the practice of not drinking and driving.

Mindful of the strong lobby for the introduction of Breathalyzer testing in Barbados, I hasten to caution that irrespective of the purpose for which it is intended to serve, careful thought must be given to its introduction and implementation as far as respecting the rights of the the individual is concerned.

Moving to the implementation phase, those entrusted with the management of such a programme, must so execute their actions that they win and maintain the respect and confidence of the general public.

CTUSAB takes this opportunity to laud the continued efforts of NCPAD and the NCSA against drug abuse in all its forms. I can assure you that the Congress recognizes the value of your efforts, as it is considered that these complement those of the labour movement, in promoting a safety and health culture in the workplace.

Remarks by Dennis de Peiza, General Secretary, CTUSAB,
National Committee for the Prevention of Alcoholism and Drugs Dependency, Breathalyzer Seminar.
June 26th, 2003, National Union of Public Workers

Chapter Five

Rights And Responsibilities

Each Individual Should Be Responsible for His/Her Actions

I consider it a distinct privilege and a pleasure to join you here at St. Judes this evening to share in your week of celebrations. Moreso, I welcome the opportunity to speak to you on what I consider to be a most appropriate theme.

Seventy-two hours ago, as I preoccupied myself with the celebrations to mark Teachers Week 2000, I never for a moment conceived that I would be called upon to be here. However I see this as another opportunity for me to contribute to the educational upliftment of members of this society, and by extension to their wholistic development.

Before proceeding further, let me thank Rev. Maxwell for consenting to have me here this evening as a replacement for Ms. Sandra Mason, who was originally slated to address you. Unfortunately, she had to leave the island urgently on government business. It would be remiss of me should I fail to acknowledge the confidence that Ms.

Mason, my colleague on the National Committee for Monitoring the Rights of the Child, has placed in me, having recommended me as her replacement.

It is my understanding that during the course of the week you have been blessed with some excellent presentations. It is my hope that at the end of the evening that the quality of my presentation would have met your expectations. In setting the framework for my presentation, let's first establish that rights and responsibilities are associated with persons of all ages. I associate these two elements with the well known cliché, "from the womb to the tomb". Hence rights and responsibilities will feature wherever man exists on the planet earth.

Firstly, I wish to establish that a high premium is placed on defending and protecting whatever rights man perceives he has, as determined by convention and or law. In my opinion it would seem that the same high premium is not placed by man in meeting the expectations of society, which it determines are his responsibilities.

When one thinks about responsibilities, one might even venture to categorize them as impositions, because of the demands they make on the individual. It might be logical to conclude that responsibilities are more graciously accepted and mean more to many when there are clear signals that benefits and rewards are to be achieved. In searching for an answer as to how people view rights and responsibilities, I sought to play a little mind game as I prepared myself for this exercise. I therefore wondered what the response would be like if I posed this open question to the audience : 'What does each individual consider as his/her rights as a citizen of Barbados?'

Something tells me that I could expect a multiplicity of responses to that question. Moreso than anything else, I anticipated that each individual would see it as part of his/her responsibility to remind me of their constitutional rights.

On the other hand, if I were to pose the question of 'What are your responsibilities as a citizen of Barbados? I suspect that the responses would be slow in coming as most persons would stop to ponder over the question as if it were the most difficult ever posed.

In this contemporary era, it has not become uncommon to hear almost every individual, group or organization, speaking to the question, of its rights. What do we really mean when we speak of 'our rights'?

According to the Oxford Universal Dictionary, our rights are simply our entitlements. In layman's language, that is, what one is lawfully due. A more academic definition would refer to rights as 'A set of conditions which govern aspects of human behaviour to enable development, and the maintenance of life.'

Although both definitions reflect what our rights are, the latter seems to gel with the school of thought that rights within our society emerge out of our convention and traditions. It more or less highlights why the socialization process becomes important in maintaining the pillars on which the society has been built. It is through the process of inculcation that the norms, mores and folkways are safeguarded, and that our value system and unwritten rights are preserved.

As a Christian society, there is an acceptance and appreciation of the fact that there are some God given rights, such as the right to life.

This apart, it ought not to be missed that some rights are procured through the enactment of law. This means that regulatory systems of control are brought to bear.

Our rights, however, don't stand alone, for it should be clear that if we have the right to life, then equally so, there must be the responsibility to preserve it. In the regulation of society, our perceived rights in life are controlled by the call for accountability, as determined by the Ten Commandments in the Bible.

In moving to establish a link between rights and responsibility, I call your attention to the definition of responsibility. The Universal Oxford Dictionary defines responsibility 'as being accountable for one's action'. A broader definition refers to responsibilities as 'the discharge of rights through social, economic and political organizations, which seek to uphold them.'

Let me use a simple illustration to make the point that with the rights automatically come responsibilities. As we all know, every individual in Barbados has the right to an education, as well as to work in order to support himself and his family. Here we find a school leaver who having left school, enters the world of work, only to be found wanting. This individual infrequently attended school and exited with no academic qualifications and technical skills. The reaction of the individual to his/her dilemma is that the world has robbed him of something.

Individuals who find themselves in this position go into a denial syndrome and fail to take responsibility for their actions in not making full use of the legitimate right to a free education. They fail in accepting the responsibility for not preparing themselves for the world of work on the completion of school life. Is it fair then for any individual to blame society for his/her failure?

Using the outcomes of this example as a guide, we should come to recognize that responsibilities emerge out of a framework of laws and regulations that govern how actions are to be carried out. Often, responsibilities are left to the individual, who may be unaware of what underpins their role in carrying out or maintaining one's responsibility.

If this is applied to what exists in our Barbadian community, where individuals and groups seek to play ignorant of what their responsibilities are to themselves and the wider society, while at the same time passing on the blame for their shortcomings to others, then it is not difficult to understand why there is a social crisis in our society today.

Out of this emerges the issue of the abuse of what is perceived as a given right. The abuse of one's rights can be taken from one extreme to another. There are those who show no regard for hard fought and earned rights, while there are others who believe that because they have a right, that they could exercise it without regard for our laws, customs, practices and traditions.

Take for instance the struggles of our forefathers as slaves from Africa to gain their freedom from our European masters, as well as those of our other pioneers who fought to secure these rights. We as a people now have a responsibility to defend, protect and preserve them.

When some young and old people alike choose not to exercise the right to vote in a general election, they fail in discharging a responsibility to themselves and to the state by not participating in the collective decision making process, in determining who should govern.

It would appear that some of us neither treasure the right that we have, or the responsibility to discharge it.

Earlier I alluded to the fact that in many instances, society takes its rights for granted. As a result, persons in exercising their civic, constitutional, personal and spiritual rights, take a lot of latitude, based on interpretations of the unwritten and written conventions and statutes of law.

Many of the actions on the part of some individuals and sections of our community, come out of their strong sense of belief that the constitution of Barbados grants them absolute freedom. Since there is no such thing as absolute freedom, the freedom of each individual is constrained by law. To stress the point, no citizen regardless of age, class, colour, race or gender is above the law.

Therefore the guarantee of the right to freedom of speech and expression, freedom of association and assembly, freedom of religion and equality before the law, does not justify that one could do as he/she likes, without regard to how his/her action affects the rest of the society. If this were allowed to exist, then the law of the jungle would apply.

In our homes, schools, churches, youth groups and clubs, workplaces, and even within the Cabinet and Parliament of Barbados, there are established rules which all persons within that group are expected to follow. In as much that every individual has the right to be a member of a particular group with which he chooses to associate, that individual by the same token has a responsibility to uphold the rules of the group or organization. It should not be ignored that they are consequential actions that are applied when rules and regulations are broken.

What therefore, does this mean for the members of our society? It means that every individual has a responsibility to practice being a good citizen. 'What does society expects of a good citizen?' It is expected that a good citizen not only accepts the norms and values of the society in which we live, but also respects the rule of law and order. Consistent with this thinking, it is expected that any form of deviant behaviour that runs counter to what the society accepts as a standard would be denounced.

A good citizen accepts that it is his right to live in a society devoid of voilence, drugs and crime. Therefore he sees it as part of his responsibility to the society in which he lives to attack this scourge of irresponsible behaviour by giving support to the police and other legitimate social agencies, which attempt to arrest these forms of anti-social behaviour.

It is expected that every good citizen would not exploit the gift of freedom of speech to walk around and use expletives at will, without regard for others. Whilst it is the individual right to drink alcohol, is this to be taken to mean that the individual has the right to drive on our streets under the influence, without giving due regard for the life of other road users, as well as his own? Is it acceptable that an individual should be allowed to show disregard for the standards of the church and come into the holy sanctuary unseemly dressed, operating under the guise that the freedom of choice to dress within reason applies?

I put it to you that in all of these instances, there is nothing to suggest that the right of the individual stands apart from his/her responsibility to himself and others. Each individual who considers that he/she has the right to live as he chooses, also has to consider the responsibility he has to society in demonstrating that he is a role model by upholding the ideals and standards set by the society in which he lives.

In focusing upon the chaos which currently exist in our society, it is not difficult to arrive at the conclusion that much of the disorder that prevails is directly linked to the thinking which promotes individual and group rights; which more often than not bears no relation to their wider social responsibility.

There seems to be a great obsession with human rights, moral rights, political rights, labour rights and things of that nature, which are grouped or self-centred in nature, and which safeguard the interest of a select few. The current generation needs to develop a consciousness that accountability is also tied to the broad societal rights. It would appear that the responsibilities of the individual to family, community and state have either been conveniently swept under the carpet, or deliberately ignored.

As a people we can hardly ignore the fact that there is a growing imbalance in society, as it relates to the attitude, perceptions, understanding of and appreciation for what are determined as rights and responsibilities. With the new philosophies and ideologies that have emerged in some quarters, these are being seriously challenged in the same quarters. Realistically speaking, the value system of our society as we have come to know it is now under threat.

Taking an objective look at the transformation taking place in society, it begs the question: Is it enough to take a cursory glance to simply focus on whether the populace is carrying out its social responsibility in safeguarding the pillars on which society has been built?

I am of the opinion that we are further challenged to explore whether society, through the actions of its educational and the judicial systems in particular, have not contributed to the declining state of our social fabric by down-playing responsibilities and promoting rights. In looking at the realities of what is happening around us, it would seem that the state has assumed the full responsibility in meeting many of the obligations once assumed by the institution of the family. The actions of the state could sometimes amount to sending mixed signals, which could lead to a matter of complacency on the part of the populace and a dependency upon the state.

One instance of the mixed signals to which I refer, comes out of the support given to the incidence of teenage pregnancy. Following the United Nations Declarations on The Rights of The Child, the state in recognizing the right of every child to an education, has seen it as its responsibility to ensure that teenage girls who become pregnant while still at school are not denied the right to pursue their education.

As you are well aware the boys as potential fathers, remain in the safe zone and will continue to pursue their education as though nothing has happened. Those girls who stay on the fringe of the law and become pregnant at age sixteen, and even those who are under the legal age of consent, would readily state their claim to the right to re-enter school.

The state, in exercising its responsibility, is placed in a compromising position. It has to face up to the condemnation of the behaviour of the offenders by the church, which perceives these actions to be morally wrong. Considering that many of those of child-bearing age are juveniles, is the state in turn to be rightly accused of supporting child abuse?

I must point out to you, the fact that many of the fathers are usually adults who are not brought to justice. It seems to me that the latitude extended to our youth gives the feeling of comfort and the licence for them to continue in their lifestyle, without having to account for their behaviour. The fact that the state is called upon through its welfare agencies to assist in the financial support of the children, speaks to the irresponsible behaviour of our men, young and old alike, in meeting the responsibility of fatherhood.

The references to which I have alluded, accurately reflect the indifference that has pervaded our society, with respect to how our people respond to their rights and responsibilities. Whereas the provisions of rights are laudable, what evidence is there to support the view that we are encouraging our youth to accept some responsibility for their action? I would argue that we are supporting the development of a social dilemma.

In closing, it is clear to me that the society has to make a more conscious effort to demonstrate that it is its brother's keeper. Each and every individual must be called upon to recognize that no man stands on his own and whatever he does by way of perceived God-given rights, conventions or statutory rights, bear a relation to others in society. Our actions should not be directed to offend. Hence in exercising our individual rights, we should demonstrate a sense of responsibility in respecting the rights of each other. I strongly suggest that this is the only way that people will comfortably co-exist in an environment.

A topic such as this one is almost inexhaustible, but I think that I have whetted your appetite enough in order to end here.

Let me thank you for your attentiveness, and I sincerely hope that I would have succeeded in stimulating your thoughts during the course of this presentation.

> Presentation made to The St. Judes Anglican Church Patronal Festival, Friday, October 27th 2000

Absenteeism in the Public Service

The startling assertion by the Right Honorable Prime Minister of Barbados, Owen Arthur, at the opening of the 62nd Annual Delegates Conference of the Barbados Worker's Union of the high incidence of absenteeism being recorded within the Public Service, is a matter that can hardly be ignored by the trade union movement.

The commitment of the movement to promote high levels of productivity has been well established. It is our view that where there is evidence of signs of diminishing output in the employment sector that has the potential of impacting negatively on the national economy, that this should be immediately become the subject of a thorough investigation.

A report carried in one of the local daily newspapers of September 18, 2003, cited that on a daily basis as many as 150 employees were reported to be absent from duty at the Queen Elizabeth Hospital. Based on the fact that the Queen Elizabeth Hospital currently has a staff compliment of 2068 employees, and accepting that the figure quoted is accurate, then this translates into an approximate 7.25 per cent absentee rate.

Towards ensuring that the figures reflect accurately the status of absenteeism at our main health care facility, it is important that a detailed analysis is undertaken in identifying the number of employees in this 7.25 per cent who are on legitimate leave from duty, be it vacation, sick leave, maternity leave, training and/or study leave. This is important, if only to satisfy all and sundry that the figure given is not over-stated or exaggerated.

Accepting that the reported level of absenteeism is attributed to the reasons referred to above, the labour movement would be hard pressed to chide employees at that or any other workplace within the public sector, where there is no tangible evidence that there have violated their existing working conditions.

However, the Congress hastens to warn that it is not supportive of any indiscriminate action on the part of employees, which gives support to any claim that they may be abusing the system.

The right of appointed public sector employees to 21 days certificated sick leave, and temporary officers to 14 days certificated sick leave, is a noted condition of service. There can be no compromising of this. None the less, the Congress urges employees within the public and private sectors to demonstrate a sense of commitment to duty and to meaningfully contribute to the overall output of their workplace, through their quality of input and output whilst on the job.

Should Heads of Departments in the Public Sector identify with the comments of the Right Honourable Prime Minister, then there is grave cause for concern, as absenteeism would be an ugly feature to behold across the public sector of Barbados.

If by any stretch of the imagination that this was to be the case, then it would be advisable that the Government undertakes to examine the causation factors that may be contributing to the development of such a phenomenon. The question is: Is it an action related to the perceived non-transparent process as it relates to recruitment, promotion, study and training leave? Or, is it tied simply to the fact that employees are not motivated and have become disenchanted as a result of poor human resources strategies being implemented, poor management and leadership at the departmental level, poor wages and salaries being paid, and poor working conditions?

Assuming that the problem of absenteeism if it exists, is a major factor, and one that is linked to legitimate illness, then it can be addressed, if the Social Partners move to satisfy Section 5.10 of Protocol 4, which states "The Social Partners acknowledge that disabilities and absences are costly at the levels of the worker, enterprise and state, and therefore agree to cooperate to promote health awareness programmes with a view to building well-being and morale and preventing loss of worker productivity due to disability and unavoidable illness".

Dennis de Peiza, General Secretary, Congress of Trade Unions and Staff Associations of Barbados, 2003

Homosexuality and Teachers: Protection of the Rights of Gays and Lesbians

The subject of human rights is a phenomenon that continues to gain currency around the world. Many a struggle has been fought and won, particularly in relation to the rights and freedom of people of various races and ethnic backgrounds.

History will recall the black liberation struggles in the United States of America, led by the late Dr. Martin Luther King Jr., which sought to eradicate the discriminatory practices and injustices imposed against black people.

Standing on the principle that discriminatory practices should be outlawed, the lesbian and gay community of the U.S.A., has been at the forefront of a world campaign to champion the cause of lesbian and gay rights.

Fortunately this campaign has not taken root in the Caribbean.

Recently, I attended the 2nd World Congress of Education International in Washington, D.C., along with teachers from 150 nations across the globe. Not only was I surprised at the openness with which some of the 2 000 delegates and observers (teachers) in attendance identified themselves as members of the lesbian and gay community, but moreso at the fact that an overwhelming majority of delegates voted in favour of a resolution on the 'protection of the rights of lesbian and gay education personnel'.

What was most disturbing was the fact that the Executive Board of Education International, in putting forward the resolution, called for support for the right of teachers to choose whether or not to be open about their sexual orientations in the workplace.

Inasmuch as I could live with the part of the resolution that speaks against discrimination and harassment on the basis of sexual orientation, which included the denial of promotion, dismissal, unwarranted transfer, unequal treatment in labour conditions, harassment or violence against lesbian and gay teachers or education workers, it is hard to accept that teachers could be allowed to be open about their sexual preferences in the classroom. As a matter of fact, any such suggestion should be dismissed with utter contempt.

I was heartened by the fact that member units of the Caribbean Union of Teachers, who attended the Congress in their individual right as members of Educational international, not only voiced their abhorrence against that provision of the resolution referred to above, but went further and voted against it.

Based on the principle that teachers are responsible for developing the minds of our young people, instilling the norms and values which society accepts, it saddens one to think that teachers worldwide could support a resolution which encourages the promotion of lesbianism and homosexuality in the classroom.

Having accepted the fact that trade unions worldwide have a responsibility to concern themselves with the rights of people, and in particular the rights of labour, I concede that there are limits which abound all things.

In terms of teachers being open about their sexual orientation in the workplace, how far are we prepared to go? Are our societies prepared to compromise morality for the sake of identifying with the international order?

It would appear that in Europe, North, South and Latin America, lesbianism and homosexuality is accepted as a way of life. Let us not, however, get into the right and wrong of the issue, but concentrate instead on what society accepts as the practice.

As a Christian society, Barbados has never accepted lesbianism or homosexuality. This society is, however, in no position to condemn others worldwide. In the Barbadian society, one is sure to find lesbians, homosexuals and bisexuals.

As a people, we have to protect our society from such behaviours that can lead to further moral decay. Our children must not be placed in a dilemma in having to determine whether the teachings of the Bible on sexual relations between male and female is the ideal, or is a matter of choice.

I applaud every Teachers' Union from within the Caribbean region, that chose not to identify with a resolution to promote one's sexual orientation in schools.

More importantly, let us concentrate our efforts, as far as possible, towards eradicating any forms of sexual abuse in our schools, wherever it exists.

> Published: Trends Magazine - August 1998 Barbados Advocate Newspaper - September 10th, 1998. Caption: 'Homosexuality and Teachers'

Chapter Six

General Presentations

Challenge to Teachers - Observing the Professional Code of Ethics

"Colleagues:

This year's Teachers' Week is being celebrated from October 26 to November 1, 1997. In past years the week's activities have been organized by the B.U.T. This year the week's activities are being jointly organized by the Barbados Union of Teachers and the Barbados Secondary Teachers' Union.

As is customary at this time of year, our nation's attention is brought to focus on the all-important subject of education. As the public's attention is captured during this period, the opportunity is seized to highlight the significance of our educational system to national development. At the same time, the teaching profession is afforded the opportunity to promote and project itself.

On the eve of Teachers' Week celebrations, teachers today are observing Teachers' Professional Day. This is an important day for members of the profession, inasmuch as they recognize the need to engage themselves in professional upliftment activities. Their deliberations which will focus on strategic planning, are undoubtedly aimed at improvements in the teaching and learning process.

Today, I call upon all teachers in our educational system to recommit themselves once again to the career of their choice, and to work towards maintaining the good image of the teaching profession. I challenge each and every teacher to set and maintain high standards and to observe the code of ethics of the profession. It may not be necessary to remind you that as a professional, the aim of every teacher should be the aim at perfecting the art of teaching and to strive for excellence at all times.

Let me impress upon you, that professionalism is not simply an adjective ascribed to an individual, but rather it relates to observing the standards that the profession expects of every teacher. It means, therefore, that our professionalism will be judged by our practices, the ideals we set and standards that we uphold.

In reflecting on our role and responsibility as teachers, we must not lose sight of the influence we bring to bear in shaping the minds and lives of our nation's children. Teachers must be cognizant of the fact that our responsibility as professionals goes beyond that of the children we teach. Let us recognize our professional responsibility to our colleagues. Inasmuch that we accept and recognize that each child matters, so too does the professional upliftment of each one of our colleagues. This we can give effect to by following a collaborative and collegiate approach in the move towards assisting each other in developing and improving teaching techniques and strategies. There is therefore the need for the pooling and sharing of ideas and resources, which compliment the common professional bond.

As a body of teachers, we must aim to develop further and consolidate our professional bond by way of identifying with and cementing our relationship with our representative body. This would be consistent with our recognition of the role of the teacher trade union as a representative and professional body, whose function it is to safeguard and promote our interest. Consistent with this, is our assumed loyalty to that body. However, this does not mean that there is an automatic surrender of one's freedom to exercise options of choice, but rather the expression of the choice in the context of a functioning democracy.

What needs to be clearly understood is that whatever action that we choose to display as individuals or as a group, should not serve to threaten the organization's stability or undermine it; thus calling its integrity into question. In short, we should not be party to any form of behaviour which subjects our organization to public ridicule, as a means to an end of sufficing one's immediate interest.

Professionalism therefore, is not about projecting, of one's expertise in educational matters, or masquerading oneself publicly as a loyalist to the cause of education of our nation's children, but more so should be reflected in the consistency of our behaviour as teachers and as members of a professional organization representing teachers. This is the only way that teachers as professionals can gain the respect and support of the public.

Finally, as we take a broader look at ourselves as professionals, be reminded that as members of a trade union which has a pedagogical and syndical focus, we owe it to ourselves to stand up for certain principals.

Therefore, paramount to all other things, we should always side on the principle of any issue, since this, as the rule of thumb, should never be compromised. On the subject of our professional status, we should maintain that the value of our contribution to nation-building should be reflected in better pay and conditions of work. As professionals, we must demand that we be properly treated and given the respect we rightly deserve. Colleagues, I urge you to press on and to continue to carry out your duties with the greatest sense of professionalism.

As you do so, continue your search for knowledge and truth."

Dennis de Peiza, President, Barbados Union of Teachers
(Address: Teachers' Professional Day, 1997)

Teaching: A Profession in Transition

"Distinguished ladies and gentlemen, colleagues and friends, welcome to "Merryhill", the home of the Barbados Union of Teachers. I am delighted to have you here this evening to participate in this evening's activity, which has become a significant event in the Annual Teachers Week Celebrations.

Let me extend a special welcome to those who are visiting with us for the first time. A warm welcome is also extended to the President and other officers of our sister union, the Barbados Secondary Teachers' Union.

Having the privilege of being your host for this evening, I endeavour to live up to the high standards set by my predecessors. Those who have had the pleasure of being with us on such an occasion, would attest to the excellent hospitality for which the B.U.T. is known. You can be sure to receive the same level of hospitality this evening.

It is not my intention to limit the extent of socializing this evening, but I implore you to grant me your attention for a few moments, as I make some observations.

Speaking specifically to this week's celebrations, I must suggest to you, that there is something special about it. It is made special by virtue of the fact that for the first time representatives of the B.U.T. and B.S.T.U. formed a committee to plan the week's activities. The committee even went further and addressed other activities, which formed part of the "Educational Month" Celebrations. This is a significant development in the movement towards establishing closer ties between the two unions.

You may recall that on assuming the office of President of the B.U.T., I voiced the hope that the two unions would move towards a closer working relationship as a means of expediting the process of unification. I can safely say that all indications point to the fact that we are seemingly well on our way.

It would seem however, that there are serious attempts from external sources to test the unions' readiness and willingness to work as one. Considering the major developments which have surfaced in education circles and recognizing the need for greater vigilance by the teachers unions, it would appear as though the character of both unions is under severe scrutiny, as elements in our society attempt to assess their maturity to fight issues together.

In focusing on the theme for Teachers' Week 1997, 'Teaching, A profession in Transition', one only has to critically assess the changes which are being introduced in education today, and make valid judgments on their impact on the teaching profession.

The profession is under serious stress as it attempts to come to grips with the many radical changes in education. Such changes include general reform in education, changes in conditions of service, and the introduction of computers in schools, under the Edutech 2000 Programme. Unfortunately much of this is taking place without adequate consultation and negotiation with the teachers unions.

The public bashing which the profession has been subjected to over the past decade and more so of late, from various quarters including the Ministry of Education, has done little to advance the cause of the profession. It has done irreparable damage to the profession, which was once held in high esteem.

Teachers have become more reserved and withdrawn and are seemingly operating under apprehension. They look to their representative and professional bodies in teachers' unions for support in protecting their interests in a rapidly changing educational environment, which I must reiterate demands a lot more of the teacher. The efforts of the teachers' union to ensure that the system does not make unjustified demands on their members have been seriously challenged. This extends to the point that the unions themselves also feel threatened. Surely, the trade union has a right of response on legitimate trade union issues without the innuendoes and attacks from responsible members of the public.

The B.U.T. and the B.S.T.U. must therefore not allow themselves to be sidetracked by provocative statements, but rather continue to focus on the business before hand by providing quality representation and fighting issues on a matter of principle. Indeed the unions must resist attempts to divide their memberships. Groupings within the unions need to recognize that to further fragment themselves is to weaken the cause of the profession. There must be a recognition of the fact that the strength of any union lies within its numbers and the stability of the organization.

As I close, let me thank Mr. Cobin Hinds, chairman of the Teachers' Week Planning Committee, as well as the other members of this committee, for their hard work in organizing the many activities for this week's celebrations. I will take this opportunity to extend a special invitation to you to attend the inaugural John Cumberbatch Memorial Lecture that will be delivered by Mr. Harcourt "Harry"

Husbands, on Wednesday, October 29, at the Sir Hugh Springer Auditorium, Solidarity House. Our Cultural Evening takes place on Friday at Solidarity House – 8:00 p.m. The Arts and Craft exhibition will be staged at the Grand Salle, Central Bank Building, and the Barbecue and Fish Fry is scheduled for Saturday evening.

I sincerely hope that you will enjoy the remainder of the evening, as you mingle and enjoy the hospitality of the Barbados Union of Teachers.

I thank you."

>Remarks delivered at the BUT's President Reception, Teachers' Week, 1997; Dennis de Peiza, President

Gender Relations - Its Implications for Teaching

"Today, it is my distinct pleasure to welcome you, the participants and presenters to this workshop, organized by the Women's Affair Committee of the Barbados Union of Teachers.

This seminar is being staged to mark the celebration of International Women's Day, 1998.

I am pleased at the fact that the Committee has chosen as the theme of the seminar: 'Gender Relations, its implications for teaching.' This to my mind is significant since there is a need to move beyond the focus of women's issues to the wider subject of gender issues.

Accepting that the problems which confront us in our daily lives affect the lives of both sexes, we must acknowledge that how society develops, depends largely on how it is shaped by the people within it.

It is therefore necessary for us, as educators, to impress upon the young citizens of this land, the importance of having a balanced outlook on life. It becomes essential to promote equality, cooperation and an understanding of the roles of both sexes, if our society is to move forward with our males and females rising to meet the challenges of responsibility.

If we accept the notion of equality within our society, then it suggests that today's exercise should direct our attention towards assessing whether there is a need for a redefining of the role of the school in the socialization process. Today's discussions should also challenge us to address the subject of gender biases, as it relates to the implications these hold for teaching.

Accepting that over time there have been drastic changes within education, today's discussion would be incomplete if we failed to examine why teaching no longer attracts a high percentage of male teachers as in earlier years. The discussions should also zero in on the significance and impact of the change to the system of co-education.

I anticipate that today's experience will be an extremely interesting one, which is characterized by intense and lively debate. On behalf of the Women's Affairs Committee, thank you for being here to participate in this seminar. I am sure at the end of the day, the ideas generated and conclusions reached will be of immense significance, and would lead towards a better understanding of the gender issues within the realm of education."

Welcome Remarks B.U.T Sponsored One Day Women's Seminar
Dennis de Peiza, President, Barbados Union of Teachers

Promoting Improved Labour Management Relations

"I am indeed honoured this morning to address you at the start of such an important workshop. It was intended that Senator Sir Roy Trotman, President of CTUSAB would have been here to address you. At this time he is currently in Geneva attending meetings of the ILO Governing Body.

Let me take this opportunity to convey to you his appreciation for the ongoing efforts of all concerned in the promotion of PROMALCO as a new strategy to workplace management relations.

I wish to express thanks to the Labour Department for having extended an invitation to the Congress of Trade Unions and Staff Associations to participate in this 'Train the Trainers' Workshop. In the same vein, the Labour Department and indeed the Ministry of Labour must be credited for taking a lead role in moving the process forward in Barbados. I must say that this approach is what is needed throughout the Caribbean, if the required change is to come about.

We in the labour movement consider that in the promotion of improved Labour Management Relations, it is becoming increasingly important to have the stakeholders, namely the employers, workers, government and the trade unions, identifying with fora such as this one. Furthermore, the leadership role they play in giving vent to such an initiative is equally as important.

As you would appreciate, the idea of improved Labour Management

Relations is one that holds immense significance for CTUSAB, in as much that the Congress has been in the forefront of promoting the tripartite approach to workplace management relations. This speaks to the development of a consultative process, which involves the employer, the employees and the trade union as the workers representative in continued social dialogue.

This process is linked to the empowerment of employees, the development of a process of consultation between employer and employees, and the participation of employees in decision-making at various levels of their various enterprises.

It is accepted that the PROMALCO initiative is tied to enhancing productivity. This is driven by the increasing nature of international competitiveness. However, we must not ignore the fact that this initiative also seeks to promote improvements in human resource management strategies, the development of bench marking systems, increasing trust in the workplace, improvements in conflict prevention, management and resolution.

If this initiative is to be successful, there must be a recognition of the fact that the process speaks to cooperation and partnership. I therefore caution that if any of the stakeholders fail to recognize this, then their actions would certainly serve to undermine the cause of maximizing the potential of the region through the use of its human resource.

It is therefore imperative that both labour and management realize the importance of their roles as they seek to achieve the goal of building better labour management relations, of which both parties stand to benefit. Indeed the end product would be reflected in the empowerment of workers and the improvement of workplace productivity.

With the coming into being of the phenomenon known as globalization, the introduction of the PROMALCO initiative could not have been more timely. Rather, this initiative must not be seen as an ad hoc or short-term measure to meet the challenges of globalization and the competitiveness associated with it. It should be embraced and sustained, not only as a means of enhancing productivity, but also as a sure way towards promoting and developing a culture of industrial harmony in the workplace, and in building social capital which is important in economic development.

Failure to recognize this by all stakeholders, and particularly the employers, would be to signal that there is a grave misunderstanding of what PROMALCO is all about and what it sets out to achieve. It is my hope that at the end of this 'Train the Trainers Workshop', there would be a better understanding of the work to be done, if we are to achieve the ultimate goal of promoting consultative and participatory mechanisms in the work place. Added to this, it should also stimulate the minds of all stakeholders that the changing global economic order demands that we change the way that we do business.

More over, it should highlight the fact that the reform process should center on the introduction of new compensation schemes that are designed towards creating a stimulus to workers' productivity, by relating individual performance to the performance of the workplace.

Such schemes are dependent on trust because they can only be implemented successfully where management provides the necessary information, and workers are prepared to accept the credibility of the information. The aim should be to encourage workplaces that pursue a decent work agenda based on the four pillars established by the ILO, which are: freedom of association, social protection, equity and social dialogue.

We wish the facilitators, resource persons and the participants a fruitful workshop, and look forward to this training being spread to many others in the near future."

Remarks To The PROMALCO Train The Trainers Workshop, June 18, 2003; Dennis de Peiza, General Secretary, Congress of Trade Unions and Staff Association of Barbados.

Globalisation: A Challenge to Remain Competitive

"Let me start by welcoming all participants to the seminar on the all important subject on the Link between Labour Standards and Productivity and Competitiveness.

I extend a special welcome to Dr. André Vincent Henry, Director of PROMALCO and

Mr. Shane Kisson, project officer, PROMALCO, facilitators for today's seminar.

Assembled here today are representatives drawn from the Social Partnership here in Barbados, to examine three fundamental aspects that are linked to the repositioning of our economy in a global changing environment.

This seminar is significant in helping all players to create a better understanding of the challenge we face with the advent of globalisation, and to develop the type of relationship that is necessary in creating an environment, which would enable Barbados to be a viable player in the world market place.

The exercise which we undertake today comes out of a change in the world economic order that forces us to change the way business was formerly done, particularly in the trading, distributive, banking and other financial service sectors.

It is important to note that both regionalization and the globalisation of markets challenge the entire Caribbean to improve productivity, and to produce high quality goods and services, if it is to remain competitive.

The bottom line is that this demands a change of approach and attitude on the part of both management and labour. It means that it is imperatitive that a highly trained, creative, disciplined and motivated work force must be developed, if Barbados and the entire region is to compete meaningful in the global market place.

The development of Labour Codes which are labour centred and that are aimed at providing better conditions of work and promoting better employment practices, are desirable, This is paramount if trust is to be developed between employer and employee; towards building better workplace relationships and a stimulating a highly motivated and productive labour force.

To re-emphasise the point, it is anticipated that where good workplace relationships exist, this would easily be translated in greater efficiency and productivity.

Accepting that increase output and efficiency serve to position businesses to be far more competitive, it stands to reason that the output of labour would be tied to the inputs that employers make to motivate their employees. Hence there is the need for employers to identify clear productivity standards.

From a labour perspective, today's seminar ought to impress upon Private Sector Employers and Government (as an employer), that should they fail to work together towards putting systems in place that are aimed at developing Labour Management Communication and Cooperation, and promoting the interest of workers as an important partner, then this could prove disastrous in maintaining high levels of productivity, as well as being competitive.

Finally, let me recognize the efforts of the Labour Department, and in particular the work of the local PROMALCO Task Force under the chairmanship of Mr. Vincent Burnett, for the work it is doing in sensitising and training members of the Social Partners in Barbados about the PROMALCO Initiative.

It is my hope that these efforts will be intensified towards reaching those in the top management positions in the business community, if the inevitable change to the new way business is to be done, is to become more apparent.

Remarks to the National Tripartite Seminar on the link between Labour Standards and Productivity and Competitiveness, BWU Labour College, June 30th, 2003

Dennis de Peiza, General Secretary, Congress of Trade Unions and Staff Associations of Barbados.

Challenge to Workers and Management - "Advancement Tied to Excellence"

"The pleasure is mine this evening to bring greetings on the behalf of the Congress of Trade Unions and Staff Association on this occasion to mark the beginning of Hotel & Restaurant Week 2003.

It is only fitting that I extend thanks to the Barbados Workers Union through its Hotel and Restaurant Division, for the invitation extended to the Congress to participate in this evening's proceedings.

Let me at the outset Mr. Chairman, commend and congratulate Comrade LeVere Richards and his team on their continued efforts in promoting the work of Hotel & Restaurant Division of the Barbados Workers Union.

I have observed that this division is a flag bearer in promoting the ideal of regionalism, inasmuch that it is known to extend invitations to its counterparts from across the region to participate in the annual celebrations.

Further, the division's annual tour to a selected Caribbean island reflects its commitment towards promoting and developing a bond among colleagues across the region. It is my understanding that there are some visiting Caribbean brothers and sisters with us this evening, and so in the true Barbadian spirit, I extend a hearty welcome to you.

Turning my attention to the theme for this year's week, 'Advancement through workers excellence', I considered it as being appropriately linked to the idea of promoting excellence in the workplace.

Ladies and gentlemen, as you would recall, in the month of March this year, here in Barbados there was the celebration of the Week of Excellence. This idea, which was the brainchild of John Agard of the BWU, was piloted through the Congress of Trade Unions.

In today's working environment where competitiveness rules supreme, there can be no doubt that advancement is tied to excellence. Efficiency, high quality output, a highly trained and motivated workforce and best management and workplace practices, are all the main ingredients for achieving advancement through workers excellence.

It is a challenge to both workers and management to strive to achieve excellence, if meaningful advancement is to be made at the enterprise and/or sectoral level.

It is important that management and workers see that advancement in the form of growth and development is tied to the way business is done.

It is therefore important that we continue to recognize that the purpose of business is to get and keep customers. The business of serving people as you do in the hotel and restaurant sector, should remain at the forefront of whatever you do, as your personal economic well-being and the growth of national economy are dependent on it.

Workers therefore ought to be mindful that excellence and

advancement could be achieved if people like their place of work, enjoy coming to work, enjoy working with their colleagues who cooperate and share the same goals or compelling vision, listen to and help each other, and enjoy job satisfaction.

The employer and management should be aware that advancement through workers' excellence could be assured if the work environment sustains enthusiasm, promotes creativity and encourages workers to go the extra mile, and allows for staff input that is regularly sought and that is acted upon. If this is to be achieved, then there must be strong and proactive leadership, and employer accountability.

I must stress that in order to strive to achieve advancement through excellence, employers must promote ongoing training towards realizing staff learning and development. Equally so, they must provide opportunities for workers' involvement and empowerment.

There must be recognition of individual and team achievement. Mechanisms ought to be put in place to stimulate productivity, develop staff morale and ensure the retention of staff. In like manner, systems should be established to develop a performance workplace, which ensures accountability for results.

Finally, I must stress the need for progressive employer-employee relations. There ought to be an environment that fosters a positive collaborative employer-employee relationship, which addresses that all employees are treated fairly. It is through this means that trust and respect will develop. I strongly suggest that trust and mutual respect are the fundamentals that will drive the process leading to 'advancement through workers excellence'.

It is now left for me to extend best wishes to you for a productive and enjoyable week of activities."

Dennis de Peiza, General Secretary, Congress of Trade Unions and Staff Associations of Barbados, August 30th, 2003.

Fraternal Greetings to the Barbados Workers Union 62nd Annual Delegates Conference

"Mr. Chairman, Mr. President General, Right Honourable Prime Minister, Owen Arthur, Senator Sir Roy Trotman, other distinguished members of the platform party, members of the diplomatic corps, members of the Social Partnership, delegates and observers, ladies and gentleman.

On behalf of the Congress of Trade Unions and Staff Associations of Barbados, I bring greetings this morning to this 62nd Annual Delegates' Conference of the Barbados Workers Union.

In an era characterized by the building of partnerships, it comes as no surprise to us in the Congress that the BWU has chosen to direct the focus of this conference to 'Investing in Relationships'. I may add that this is consistent with the labour movement's vision of developing interlocking relationships towards creating social cohesion, in addition to creating a platform which serves to advance the economic development of Barbados.

Further, I suggest that the experience of the labour movement coming out of the workings of the Social Partnership in Barbados, is enough to propel unions and staff associations to continue to seek to develop relationships which would serve to advance their own agendas, as well as that of the national good.

As the movement proceeds on this path, it ought to maintain the high road approach that centers on the holistic approach to national development; one that is driven by the process of collaboration and a spirit of cooperation. Today's conference challenges you, the delegates, to address some fundamental issues of national and regional significance arising out of the CSME. CTUSAB is mindful of the many challenges that the CSME, globalisation and trade liberalization will bring.

In advocating a proactive approach in meeting these challenges, it is supportive of dialogue initiated by its affiliates in guiding the leadership in determining a policy position, and strategies that the labour movement should employ in addressing these new initiatives.

As you deliberate on the issue of the CSME, I urge you to focus on the inherent changes of this new policy initiative, which it is anticipated, will impact on the Caribbean labour market services, the quality and way of life of Barbadians and the Caribbean people on a whole. It is important that this conference considers the fall out emerging from the growing incidence of lay offs and redundancies brought about by closures and/or mergers, the exploitation of and violation of the rights of migrant labour, and the matter of the brain drain.

I would take the liberty to suggest to you, the delegates, that this is your opportunity in the participatory representation process to guide your leadership in how best to meet the pending socio-economic and political challenges that lie on your doorstep. Further, to clearly articulate your views on the best approaches to be followed in preparing Barbadian labour to meet the new challenges, in addition to identifying strategies aimed at protecting and safeguarding the interest of labour and that of the people of the Barbados and the wider Caribbean, in this drastic changing environment.

I extend best wishes for a successful conference and assure you that the Congress looks forward to the outcomes of the deliberations to follow.

Mr. Chairman, I am obliged to you."

Dennis de Peiza, General Secretary, Congress of Trade Unions and Staff Associations of Barbados.

Honour for Sir Roy

"Mr. Master of Ceremonies, distinguished Guest of Honour Senator Sir Roy Trotman, Right Honourable Prime Minister, distinguished members of the head table, distinguished guests, members of the media, ladies and gentlemen.

As the curtain begins to fall on this the Inaugural Annual Awards Dinner and Ball of the Congress of Trade Unions and Staff Associations of Barbados, I believe that it is appropriate to close the evening's proceedings in like manner as we commenced.

Let me therefore start citing the first and last verses of Hymn 379 Ancient and Modern Hymn Book, which go like this:

"Now thank we all our God,
With heart and hands and voices,
Who wondrous things hath done,
In whom his world rejoices,
Who from our mothers' arms
Hath blessed us on our way,
With countless gifts of love,
And still is ours today.

All praise and thanks to God,
The father now be given,
The Son and him
With them in highest heaven,
The one eternal God,

Whom earth and heaven adore,
For thus it was, is now
And shall be ever more."

It is my belief that the two stanzas of this hymn, fittingly put into context and summarize the nature of this evening's event. This occasion that has been one of celebration, has indeed, I believe lived up to its expectations. It is my hope that we will all leave this hall with the fondest memories of a memorable evening.

As chairman of the Organizing Committee I cannot but express how elated I am that this event has been well-received. The excellent attendance we have here this evening is testimony to this fact. I speak for the members of the Organizing Committee in thanking you, our patrons, for your support for this event.

This evening we assembled here at this now renown event, to recognise the achievement of a distinguished son of the soil, in the person of Senator Sir Roy Trotman. We in the labour movement placed a premium on quality leadership, and I am happy to say that it is this quality leadership that has led Senator Sir Roy to be recognized at home and abroad as a distinguished labour leader.

We in the Congress of Trade Unions and Staff Associations of Barbados are indeed grateful that we have been afforded the opportunity during the lifetime of Senator Sir Roy, to publicly thank him for his efforts in championing the cause of labour across the length and breadth of the universe, and of course for his leadership of CTUSAB, and that of the Barbados Workers' Union.

It is to be acknowledged that commitment to the cause of the people, as we in public life all know, comes at much personal sacrifice. It is only fitting that on this occasion that I take the liberty on behalf of the workers' movement of Barbados, to in absentia, extend thanks and gratitude to Margaret, Lady Trotman, wife of Sir Roy, and to his children, for the support that they would have given to him over the years.

This evening we have been graced with the presence of a number of distinguished persons. It has been an honour to have with us, the Right Honourable Prime Minister, Owen Arthur; the Leader of the Opposition, Honourable Clyde Mascoll and Mrs. Mascoll; Honourable Reginald Farley, chairman of the Sub-Committee of the Social Partners; Senator John Williams, Minister of State in the Prime Minister's Office; Honourable Trevor A. Prescod, MP and Acting Minister of Labour and Social Security; Senator Allan Fields, Head of the Private Sector Agency; Sir John Stanley Goddard, and Pauline, Lady Walcott.

On behalf of the Organizing Committee we thank you for having graced us with your presence on this occasion.

At this time, I wish to recognize the presence of two other distinguished guests who have travelled from their base in Trinidad and Tobago to join us this evening. I refer to Mr. Brother George DePena, Secretary General of the Caribbean Congress of Labour, and Sister Paula Robinson, ILO Workers Specialist, Caribbean Office. I thank you both for being here.

This evening we have heard from the Right Honourable Prime Minister, Senator. Allan Fields, Brothers Robert 'Bobby' Morris and Patrick Frost, all of whom have paid glowing tributes to the work and achievements of Senator Sir Roy.

I must record our collective appreciation to the speakers for their kind sentiments expressed to Senator Sir Roy. I am sure that these sentiments will serve to stimulate and rejuvenate Senator Sir Roy as he continues to champion the cause of labour.

Earlier this evening Senator Sir Roy found himself on stage to receive a lifetime momento. To assist him in unveiling what laid hidden from our eyes, was Pauline Lady Walcott and Mrs. Peggy Rickinson. I am sure that you would agree that they were both gracious in undertaking the task assigned to them, and if I may add, their presence would have served as a calming influence to Senator Sir Roy's nerves at the time. We commend Pauline, Lady Walcott and Mrs. Peggy Rickinson for a job well done.

The name Jason Hope of Hope's Designs Group, must now be a household name that is synonymous with the production of artistic works that are of the highest quality. Those of us, who have seen the statue of the Right Excellent Sir Frank Leslie Walcott, would immediately come to expect nothing less than an excellent, finished product. This evening, Mr. Hope's unique artistic flair was captured in the lifetime momento that was presented to Senator Sir Roy. I am sure you will agree that Jason deserves our accolades for the work done. Let me also credit him for the work done in the coordination of the video presentations you witnessed earlier.

At the risk of speaking out of place on this occasion, I must nonetheless express hope (no pun intended), that some effort would be made at ensuring that this young talented Barbadian is given the opportunity to avail himself of training overseas, towards assisting him in developing the potential he obviously possesses.

As you would appreciate an event of this magnitude could not have been staged without the support of several persons and organizations. In the interest of time I will not attempt to identify this extensive list. Nonetheless, I take this opportunity to thank each individual, agency and/or organization that has contributed to the staging and ultimate success of this Inaugural Annual Awards Dinner and Ball.

I refer you to the copy of your programme, where you will find a list of the names of contributors to this event.

To Corporate Barbados and other organizations, I thank you for having supported this event through the purchase of corporate tables. In the same vein, gratitude is extended to all affiliates of CTUSAB for their support.

To you who purchased individual tickets to be part of this event, your attendance and support is also appreciated.

This evening no group of individuals is better placed for the highest commendation for a job well done than the members of the Organizing Committee. I cannot but salute the members on their commitment and untiring efforts to ensure that this evening was a success.

The members of the Committee are: Bros. Michael Hinds, Alwin Adams, Orlando 'Gabby' Scott, Washbrook Bayne, Jason Hope, Sisters Jeanette Brathwaite and Verneta Durant, Sis. Grace Hall, Karen Sheridan, Marcia Cumberbatch.

Ex-officio members Bros. Levere Richards and Vere Rock.

Ladies and Gentlemen I present to you the organizing committee.

Let me at this time recognize and thank Bro. Levere Richards, Ex-Officio member of the committee and Head Usher for his invaluable assistance rendered to the Organizing Committee. To the ushers, thank you for having volunteered your services and for the marvelous job you have done this evening.

To Canon Frank Marshall, Brothers Colin Norville and Desmond Weekes, we record our thanks and appreciation for your participation in this evening's proceedings.

In closing, let me thank the Executive Board of CTUSAB for having accepted my idea for the staging of this Awards Dinner and Ball and the Solidarity Concert, which preceded this event, to form part of its annual calendar of events.

I call your attention to the fact that this Inaugural Annual Awards Dinner and Ball has been initiated as the vehicle to be used for honouring those who have made a significant contribution to the cause of labour in Barbados. It is hoped that as it develops that the other members of the Social Partnership will seek to partner CTUSAB in this initiative.

Mr. Master of Ceremonies, it is now left for me to thank you for guiding us through the evening's proceedings and to make way for you to make the final pronouncements.

Thank you all for being part of another page in history of CTUSAB. Do enjoy the remainder of the evening as you dance away until the midnight hour."

VOTE OF THANKS Delivered on the occasion of the Inaugural Annual Awards Dinner & Ball of the Congress of Trade Unions and Staff Associations of Barbados; Sherbourne Conference Centre, October 31st, 2003

ILO/CIDA Regional Child Labour Project - Labour Inspectors and Strategic Planning and Impact Framework Workshop

Over some three hundred years ago, the people of the Caribbean embarked upon a new direction, at the heart of which was the removal of all traces of exploitation of our people as workers. The platform for further change was founded on the social unrest of 1937, which led to fundamental freedoms, rights and privileges being guaranteed. Today these are clearly reflected in this island's constitution.

Following on this, it would seem that we as a people have crossed the hurdle of exploitation and oppression. However, considering that we assemble here to discuss the vexing issue of the 'Elimination and Prevention of the Worst Forms of Child Labour', this suggests to me that we still have a far way to go.

Speaking to what seemingly exists within the mainstream employment sectors in Barbados, the local trade union movement is pleased that the available evidence suggests that the incidence of child labour is not a looming phenomenon that engages its undivided attention.

This is not to say that the labour movement is oblivious to the fact that there remain pockets of child labour within the society. The

2002 Dunn's Rapid Assessment Report on Child Labour in Barbados reminds us that there are children who are working in the sex industry, and who are involved in drug trafficking.

Taking the reported rate of the spread of HIV/AIDS amongst teenagers across the Caribbean, and in Barbados in particular, and the high incidence of crime and violence that is associated with drug trafficking, which in turn has a connection with our youth, policy leaders are now charged with a greater sense of responsibility, in working to finding ways of addressing the exploitation of our young people by those who seek to use them in order to maximize the financial benefits that they wish to accrue.

Based on past legislation that has been enacted, successive Governments of Barbados are to be commended on their commitment to securing the human rights and welfare of children. Whilst it is to be noted that the Education Act in Barbados makes it mandatory for children between 5 - 16 years of age to attend school, which is said to be strictly enforced, we as a people should not be thrown into a false sense of security in believing that the exploitation of child labour does not exists within the walls of our society.

We in the Caribbean and Barbados in particular, should not feel that we are excluded from the ILO's estimates that speak to the fact that 250 million Children of ages 5 - 14 are victims of child labour around the world; tens of thousands of whom are caught in the worst forms of child labour.

Considering that Barbados falls within the 25% of the 170 ILO members' states that are signatories to Convention 182 on the Worst Forms of Child Labour, today's consultation in my opinion is a very important one. It forces us to move beyond the realm of complacency, and seriously focus on the issues of prostitution, pornography and the use of children under eighteen years of age in illicit and hazardous activities.

CTUSAB applauds the Ministry of Labour & Social Security for having hosted this workshop. The Congress views that this is in keeping with its call on Government to pursue all necessary action to eliminate the scourge of child labour.

As we debate the subject of the elimination and prevention of child labour, CTUSAB takes this opportunity to remind members of the private sector not to import items for sale or use in Barbados, where there are reasonable grounds to support the fact that child labour was used in the manufacturing or production process.

Government in demonstrating its commitment to eliminating the worse forms of child labour, not only in its own backyard but also on a global scale, should move to put monitoring systems in place, to ensure that items imported into Barbados for sale or use, are not produced with the use of child labour.

When we look at the attitude of our young people today, it seems evident that they are primarily interested in earning a quick dollar. What comes across is the fact that they seen to have little regard for conditions of service of their employment. Following on this, the point is to be emphasized that as policy makers we have a responsibility to safeguard and protect their interest.

We must not lose sight of the fact that amongst us are some unscrupulous employers who are blinded by mere self interest, and who have little regard for the principles of decent work. To drive home the point, it is not a guarded secret that there are some employers who oppose union recognition and the unionization of employees. With this being the case, labour must continue to win the support of Government in an effort to uphold fundamental human rights as provided under the Constitution of Barbados, and to ensure that the principles of decent work, and the provisions of the ILO Convention 182 are observed.

We can take some comfort in the fact that the Labour Department has the authority to conduct spot checks on enterprises to verify compliance with the law, and moreover, is empowered to take legal action against any employer who is found to have engaged under age children. However, I contend that if we are to effectively police all enterprises to ensure that there is total compliance, it is necessary that Government moves to increase the current complement of inspectors in the system.

Finally, whilst this workshop focuses on the prevention and elimination of the worst forms of child labour, I consider it equally important that attention be paid to the social factors within the society that provide a platform for some employers to engage in the callous practice of exploiting child labour. Moreover, participants should be challenged to identify strategies that can be employed to combat the abuse where it exists.

It is my wish that the deliberations to follow prove to be fruitful, and I look forward to the outcomes of this workshop.

> Remarks delivered at the ILO/CIDA Regional Labour Child Project; Dennis de Peiza, General Secretary, Congress of Trade Unions and Staff Associations of Barbados. Harcourt Lewis Training Centre, Keith Bourne Complex, November 8th, 2005.

Delivering High Quality Service

"Let me start by expressing my thanks to the Barbados Workers Union for having extended an invitation to the Congress of Trade Unions and Staff Associations of Barbados to participate in today's proceedings, which officially mark the start of Hotel & Restaurant Workers' Week 2004.

As we assemble here for yet another year, it is my hope that the significance of the occasion remains foremost in our minds. It is clear that the BWU is committed to developing the consciousness of those involved in the service and hospitality sector, to the important role they are required to play in the building of the national economy of this land.

In noting the theme for this year, 'Hospitality Workers Responding Positively Towards Achieving Service Excellence', I call your attention to the fact that the subject of service excellence is not a phenomenon that is unique to Barbados as a tourist destination. I can tell that the matter of service excellence is a concern to the authorities in far away lands as Australia and Ireland.

Let me take this opportunity to remind you that when we speak of service excellence; we are referring to 'meeting and exceeding the expectations of our clients.' To put it another way, it means delivering high - value service. Earlier I alluded to the understanding of the significance of this occasion. In placing before you how I perceive the significance of the occasion to be, I can think of no better way to communicate it to you, than by impressing upon you that in a competitive global environment, we are challenged to exceed customer expectations, as it is vital to achieving a competitive edge.

Let me use this opportunity to remind both employers and employees in the audience, and as a matter of fact wherever they are, that customer service is fundamental to sustaining growth at the enterprise. I must stress the point that if effectiveness is to be realized in the service sector, it requires an improvement in employee's attitude and behaviors, as these have an indirect impact on the bottom line. You are to be guided by the principle that 'quality service makes good business sense for the individual enterprises, because it inevitably leads to satisfied customers, repeat visitation and word of mouth promotion.'

As you, as hotel and restaurant workers seek to strive to respond positively to service excellence, I urge you to be guided by the tenants of service excellence.

Firstly, you should demonstrate professional excellence....Be approachable, and treat everyone as if he/she is the most important person.

Secondly, improve upon your level of communication...Listen to the concerns of customers, and most importantly, remember your manners.

Thirdly, check on your appearance...follow the dress code policy and practice good personal hygiene.

Fourthly, demonstrate a level of personal concern...Make a good first impression, treat others like you would like yourself to be treated, and don't forget to acknowledge and smile with your guests.

Fifthly, be efficient...In so doing be accountable for your own actions, focus on what's right, not who's right, and give extraordinary service to your customers.

I leave with you an observation made by Steven Stead, with which I am sure we can all identify. In a news article of March 2004, headlined 'World class approach critical for Scottish Tourism Industry', He wrote: "One of Scotland's greatest assets is its people, and by developing and enhancing the services which industry workers provide for the tourists, will help us to realize our ambition of making Scotland a must visit, must return destination."

On behalf of the Congress, I extend congratulations to all nominees and awardees, and extend best wishes for a successful week of activities."

The Official Opening Ceremony of the Barbados Workers Union, Hotel and Restaurant Workers' Week 2004, Solidarity House, Sunday August 8th, 2004.

Dennis de Peiza, General Secretary, Congress of Trade Unions and Staff Associations of Barbados

No Need for Complacency

"The pleasure is mine this morning to bring greetings in the name of the Congress of Trade Unions and Staff Association of Barbados, to this the 61st Annual Delegates' Conference of the Barbados Workers Union.

Today we assemble here to show our support for the tremendous work completed and the notable achievements recorded by the Barbados Workers Union on behalf of the workers, and by extension, the people of Barbados.

I am of the opinion that none of us present this morning would deny that the birth of the Barbados Workers Union in 1941 heralded the beginning of a new era in the fortunes of labour in Barbados.

The Congress of Trade Unions and Staff Association of Barbados, has benefited from the groundwork laid by the BWU, whose vision has been propelled by the dynamic leadership of the late Right Excellencies Sir Grantley Adams, Sir Hugh Springer and Sir Frank Leslie Walcott, and now continued by Comrade Senator Leroy Trotman.

As a respected organization, this union must be commended for the role it plays in the ordering of Civil Society.

I believe that everyone assembled here is familiar with the BWU's motto, 'Unity is strength, where there is no vision, the people perish'. This is seemingly the plank on which this noble institution has been built. Arguably, it has influenced the outlook and focus of other sister unions and staff associations. It is even reasonable to conclude that this informed the bonding and focus leading to the formation of CTUSAB.

As we celebrate with the BWU, let us give credit to this organization for its continued vigilance in seeking to protect the rights of workers, focusing attention on and addressing national issues, and working towards ensuring a better quality of life for all Barbadians.

I take this opportunity to advise members of the BWU not to become complacent over past achievements, but to recommit themselves to the organization and to work assiduously towards positioning the union in maintaining its high profile within the Barbadian community.

While on the subject of commitment, it is but appropriate that I use this occasion to publicly thank the BWU for its service to the

Opening of the BWU's Annual Delegates Conference

Congress. As many of you are aware, the headquarters here at Solidarity House serves as the home of CTUSAB. Since 1991 the BWU has placed its facilities and resources at the disposal of the Congress.

CTUSAB thanks its President, Comrade Senator Leroy Trotman, who, in his role as General Secretary of the BWU, has embraced the Congress in many collaborative efforts, so as to advance the cause of the umbrella body. This is testimony to the commitment of the BWU towards giving strength to the umbrella organization. The Congress welcomes this opportunity to publicly place on record its congratulations to Comrade Senator Leroy Trotman, on his elevation to the high office of the chairman of the Workers' Group of the Governing Body of the ILO. I am sure that this audience will join me in saluting this achievement, as well as to wish our dear brother, colleague and friend, every success in his tenure of office.

To you, the delegates to this Annual Conference, I offer CTUSAB's best wishes for successful deliberations. It is our hope that apart from addressing domestic issues, that you take some time out to focus on such pressing issues as the attempts in some quarters to muzzle the voice of trade union leaders, breaches of Protocol IV, and the rising level of unemployment which is, occasioned by layoffs and redundancies. I suggest that the subject of layoffs and redundancies now in evidence at PriceSmart, should engage your attention.

Mr. Chairman, ladies and gentlemen, I thank you."

The CSME and the Implications for Immigration Control

"First let me say that I count it a privilege to have been invited to attend this Breakfast Seminar, and more so, to make a presentation to such a distinguished audience. I therefore am obliged to thank your Executive Director, Mr. Ruall Harris for having extended the invitation to me to attend.

This morning, I welcome the opportunity to outline labour's perspective on the subject of 'The CSME and its implication for Immigration Control.' I have taken careful note of the fact that the Chamber has determined that the focus of today's deliberations should not concentrate solely on the negatives associated with the free movement of labour, but be advanced to look at those beneficial effects.

This to my mind is a clear indication that the Private Sector recognizes that there are underlining issues associated with the implementation of the CSME initiative which need to be identified and addressed, in ensuring that the objectives of the CSME are not compromised.

While I understand the need to focus on the beneficial effects, I must underscore the point that labour has a responsibility to focus on those areas that would tend to impact negatively on the migrant labour. It is important that labour speaks to those shortcomings, which have the potential both in the short and long term to seriously compromise labour standards, erode gains made by labour, contribute to the exploitation of migrant labour, and which in the final analysis, severely constrain potential benefits that could possibly be derived from the free movement of labour and capital.

Today the labour movement welcomes this objective discussion, which in our opinion, provides yet another opportunity to call the attention of regional governments of the need to introduce a number of protectionists policies, monitoring systems and social nets, towards protecting and safeguarding the interest of CARICOM nationals, as they undertake to work and reside in a jurisdiction of choice across the region. It is important to have in place regulations to negate actions on the part of employers that are directed at playing off nationals against non-nationals. It is equally necessary to provide safeguards that have the effect of eliminating efforts at marginalizing migrant labour, and in so doing, remove feelings of insecurity.

The Congress of Trade Unions and Staff Association of Barbados in espousing the views of the local labour movement, is on record as being a strong advocate for the free movement of Caribbean nationals. It has been in the vanguard of raising the consciousness of Barbadians of the possible pitfalls and / or shortcomings that are more than likely to manifest themselves, when the idea of the free movement of Caribbean nationals finally becomes a reality.

One would recall that Senator Sir Roy Trotman, President of CTUSAB, in calling attention to early warning signals, sought to establish the need for a register to be compiled of immigrant labour, as a first step towards in tracking the movement of migrant labour into this island of Barbados. For whatever reason(s), Sir

Roy's suggestion was put to the sword. It would seem that those who knocked the idea were not fully conscious then of the labour movement's intention to safeguard the interest of migrant labour. Taking into consideration the many issues that have arisen with the movement of Guyanese nationals into Barbados in an environment where the labour market is considered to be imperfectly regulated, it is to be appreciated that trade unions must act decisively to address all issues affecting workers.

Current concern over the influx of Guyanese nationals into the workforce of Barbados, and the dent it is apparently making on the employment of Barbadian labour, coupled with the fact that available evidence suggest that the core labour standards are not being observed by some employers as they seek to obtain a comparative advantage. There is the need to ensure that migrant labour benefits from labour inspectorate protection. Such protection would lend to migrant labour not being treated less favourably than locals, with respect to wages, safe and decent work, that would be achieved through the observance of fair labour practices.

It is a view that the free movement of labour is considered to be critical to the proper functioning of any single market and economy. Following on this, there is the reasonable expectation that the opportunity would be provided for all persons to be able to freely trade their services or skills across the region. However, the reality is that the Revised Treaty of Chaguaramas at Articles 45 and 46 provides for university graduates, artistes, media workers, musicians and sportspersons to move freely and to work without the need for work or residency permits.

It is ironic that generally skilled labour whose services are in equal demand across the region, are left out of the loop. This surely represents a serious shortcoming that opens the door for pockets of illegal movement. On the other hand, it has the potential of increasing the recruitment of contract labour, in circumstances where migrants are offered employment contracts, the provisions of which seek to deprive them of their constitutional and basic human rights. The platform is therefore set for the exploitation of labour, as those who enter the workforce from outside of this jurisdiction, are more than likely to be subjected to discrimination, exploitation and abuse.

However, it is my judgement that there is a larger problem associated with the proposed freedom of movement, which to my mind would be of interest to members of the private sector. As we understand it, the principal objectives of the CSME, speak to the unrestricted As we understand it, the principal objectives of the CSME, speak to the unrestricted movement of people and services, the unrestricted movement of capital and the right of CARICOM Nationals to set up businesses in any CARICOM country. Further to this, the CSME initiative seeks to create more business and employment opportunities and to ensure that all CARICOM nationals who wish to carry on business in any member state are not discriminated against.

Based on the limitations of those groups that are permitted to move freely, it would seem that anything less than a blanket agreement that speaks to the free movement of all categories of workers, which in this case includes businessmen, leaves the door open to the emergence of some fundamental issues that relate to discrimination being practiced within the exercise of the broad immigration policy. Are we to conclude that the small business person who does not fall into the category of that of a university graduate, a performing artiste, media worker, musician or sportsperson is to be denied unrestricted freedom of movement to ply his / her trade? Provided that this is the case, does this not run contrary to the principal objectives of the single market and economy?

Taking into consideration the need to ensure that change is not limited to a privilege few, CTUSAB sees itself further challenged to influence meaningful and not cosmetic changes that may tend to serve sectoral interests.

It is therefore labour's view that all governments across the region should agree to the removal of all barriers to freedom of movement. This is to be seen as a decisive step in moving to eliminate any anticipated fall out. This ought not to be taken to mean that there would be a wide open door policy, which is not guided by immigration controls that focus on the economic needs and labour requirements of Barbados. Far from this being the case, I strongly suggest that it is imperative that systems are developed to carefully manage and monitor the securing and exchange of human resources in determined fields.

In adopting this approach, the country would undoubtedly be better positioned to address potential problems of labour shortages; by identifying areas of need, and securing needed human resources in technical and other fields. It is important not to loose sight of the fact that this seems to be the appropriate strategy to be employed, as a means of reducing the displacement of Barbadian labour by other Caribbean nationals.

Going even further to focus on the bigger picture, it is to be observed that this approach has the added potential of contributing to the diversification of the economic activity on the island.

The fact that today there is no common position governing the region with respect to the movement of labour, future immigration policies should in essence reflect a greater measure of flexibility in giving support to the attainment of the stated objectives of the single market and economy.

The matter of unfavourable recruitment practices is not one that is to be taken lightly. It is one that brings into sharp focus the need for immigration control, specifically for the purpose of identifying one's status of residence. This is essential if the island is to guard against the entry of illegal workers. It therefore will require that greater attention is paid to the process of acquiring and managing information on the movement of foreigners across the region. This is essentially a critical and necessary process. Bearing in mind that immigration control administration focuses on the maintenance of safety and order in the society, it means that systems for monitoring the status and movement of non-nationals must be in developed, in order to guard against illegal entry.

It is therefore essential that every precaution is exercised to guard against the efforts of persons from outside of the region, who may attempt to beat the system in order to gain entry, secure residence, and finally to gain employment without the legal right to do so. Any failure to arrest this from the outset, will more than likely result in the flagrant breaches of labour laws, the depressing of labour standards and the violation of human rights.

There is also the need to focus on the ever growing problem of crime and violence, which has assumed major importance as an obstacle to development; and which has far-reaching consequences for society. It is not to be ignored that this phenomenon has tended to inhibit inflows of investments, impacted negatively on the growth of tourism, weakened the middle class through migration, and as a consequence contributed to the outflows of capital and skills.

Amongst the number of other net consequences associated with the free and mass movement of people across the region is the fact that it imposes the need for stronger vigilance and effective law enforcement in order to keep out illegal entrants. In an age characterized by terrorists' activities, the question of national security has become a front burner issue. Indeed this has occupied the attention of Commissioners of Police across the region. They remain minded of the many challenges imposed by the free movement of labour.

One of the principal challenges facing labour is that of the harmonization of labour legislation across the region. Whereas CTUSAB recognizes that some work has been done to give effect to the harmonization of laws under the Revised Treaty of Chaguaramas, it also notes that the key constraints to the development of the draft model laws, has been the shortage of lawyers, the absence of legal professionals in some countries, as well as the lack of a legal research policy.

Be that as it may, CTUSAB holds the view that with the coming on stream of the CSME, there is more than likely to be some disparity in workers rights and conditions of service, based on the fact that regional governments are not signatories to some ILO Conventions, or have not endorsed some ILO Recommendations. It is therefore imperative that all CARICOM states which embrace the CSME, move posthaste to ratify the relevant ILO Conventions and Fundamental Principles and Rights at Work. In addition, they should move to establish a mechanism to ensure that the standards are met.

Apart from addressing the observance of the fundamental rights and freedoms of all Caribbean nationals, it is equally important that a focus is placed on the consequence of mass migration, where overpopulation, the meeting of housing needs, environmental and health issues become burning issues. There is also the increasing consciousness of the added pressures on the island's social security system and social services.

All of this places an increase burden on Government to make available the financial resources to support social needs. Herein lies the added challenge to Government to be more vigilant, and to institute mechanism to control the flight of capital. Whereas the free movement of capital is beneficial to the business community, the need for regulation is necessary, recognizing the deleterious effects the flight of capital could have on the individual economy of the small island states of the Caribbean.

In conclusion it is clear that CSME opens the door for enterprises to operate along cross border lines, and hence provides the base for business development and economic diversity. However, the major challenges that come with the implementation of the CSME is for regional Governments to remove all barriers that serve to inhibit all Caribbean nationals from enjoying the right to free movement, to implement monitoring systems for the protection of immigrants, and to ensure that protectionists' measures are enshrined in CSME common legislation."

Paper presented at the Breakfast Seminar hosted by the Barbados Chamber of Commerce & Industry, Hilton Hotel, Wednesday October 26th, 2005. Dennis de Peiza, General Secretary, Congress of Trade Unions and Staff Associations of Barbados

Social Development Policy Challenge in Barbados - A New Perspective

"Today, my task is to address the subject of 'Social Development Policy Challenge in Barbados...A new Perspective.'

In laying the foundation for this presentation, I start by identifying with the notion that social policy concerns itself with human development and sustainability. I consider it as a given that social development policy should be directed at addressing the needs of deprived people in a given society, and to prevent deprivation in the future. Consistent with this, the focus of a national social development policy should be directed at poverty reduction through wealth creation, employment generation, and social integration.

In Barbados the issues of health, poverty, labour, environmental issues, constraints on women, the elderly, youth, children and vulnerable groups, all emerge as critical areas to be addressed under the social development policy agenda. Having identified the issues, Government is now challenged to go further, and identify those areas that warrant priority attention, and to determine and implement effective corrective strategies.

To my mind, social integration as it specifically relates to older persons, persons with disabilities, family and youth should be placed on the priority list. Equally so, there is the need to treat to the more long-standing issue of the growing inequalities that exists between the rich and the poor in our society. The seriousness of this is reflected in a growing consciousness of the widening and deepening of the inequality that also exists in our society, between skilled and unskilled labour.

As I understand it, a social development policy should be directed at promoting social and economic change. It therefore follows that if there is to be any bridging of the gap between the rich and the poor, then government is obligated to concentrate its efforts on a programme that seeks to sustain poverty reduction. This seems to be the logical path to pursue, if the goal of the empowerment of people and providing better life for citizens; particularly those categorized as poor and middle-income wage earners, is to be achieved.

Much is being made of the attainment of the Millennium Development Goals, and it would seem that the Barbados Government is committed to a Social Development Policy, at the forefront of which is poverty eradication. If this policy is to achieve its intended goal, then greater emphasis has to be placed on providing a more level playing field; by creating opportunities for wealth creation; thus eliminating the vast majority of the glaring disparities and inequalities that divide the population.

Government therefore out of a sense of necessity and urgency, ought to look at improving the education and health status of the poor, addressing the matter of low income housing needs, developing a meaningful land policy, and addressing the social fallout associated with unemployment and underemployment. It is critical that Government focuses its attention on job creation, human resources development and the protection of the environment. The bottom line is that Government needs to concentrate on developing a strong social policy that creates a base for sustainable growth.

When it comes to the issue of job creation, there is the need for new initiatives to be introduced. Identifying new job opportunities seems in my judgment, the most appropriate way to fight the war of unemployment and underemployment. Recognizing the increasing number of graduates coming out the University of the West Indies, Cave Hill Campus, the Samuel Jackman Prescod Polytechnic and the Barbados Community College, this demands that a proactive approach be taken to finding solutions to the immediate and long term employment problem.

From where I sit in the labour movement, it is our position that there is need for a man power survey to be conducted. This has been long overdue, and as the opportunity presents itself to review our social policy, emphasis ought to be placed on initiating a comprehensive man power survey.

Noting the wave of academic and highly skilled individuals that are graduating out of the educational system, there is clearly the need to provide quality and better paying jobs. It is the only meaningful alternative to counteract the social fallout, where persons are prepared to engage in illegal activities such as the sale of drugs, since it supposedly brings quick and large sums of cash. When we consider that fallouts associated with the drug culture, namely, social deviance, crime and violence, it is of necessity that our social policy focuses on restoring a sense of order, and a removal of subcultural activities, that place members of the society either under siege or at risk; and more over, places strain on the island's limited resources in providing a range of social services.

Turning attention to the question of a living wage, it is outrageous to expect the working poor to survive in a high priced Barbadian society, on what amounts basically to starvation wages. Realistically, how can those at the bottom, who receive weekly wages of between $200- 300, be expected to survive, taking into consideration the high cost of house rents, utilities and food? This raises the issue of a minimum wage at the sectorial and enterprise levels, which needs to be hammered out. Admittedly, there are no quick and easy solutions to be found in addressing this.

Out of this emerges the need for greater level of social dialogue that embraces all who have a vested interest. With the establishment of the Social Partnership in Barbados, the mechanism to facilitate this has already been established. There is clearly no need to reinvent the wheel, but more so, to provide greater opportunities where civil society and the Social Partners can consult on social policy issues.

The challenge is ours to follow the approach enunciated by Phil Harding, Senior Social Development Adviser of the DFID, in India. He opined, "Usually work on governance starts with government and trickles down to the people, but social development starts at the opposite direction, hence it is the need to promote complimentary of efforts."

In any review of the social development policy of Barbados, the subject of education ought to be given priority treatment. It has often been said that education is the key to one's upward mobility, and way out of poverty. In an age of technological changes, propelled by the computer and the internet, the upgrading of people's knowledge, skills and competencies are essential, if they are to be suitably placed to compete for available jobs opportunities.

Is it justifiable to speak glowingly to the fact that the literacy rate in Barbados stands at approximately 90%, that over 50% of Barbadian households have a secondary education, and over 40% have a primary education, whilst the reality is that the vast majority of our school leavers are not fit for the job market? If the claim is one hundred percent accurate that 70% of secondary school leavers in Barbados, do so without certification, and that some technical skills taught in schools are irrelevant to the labour market, then there is a need to rethink the educational component of our social policy. Greater emphasis must be placed on work place skills that embrace the new technologies.

It can be argued that in the execution of its social policy, that Government's public spending is limited by virtue of the financial resources available to it. Taking into consideration the effects of globalization, it would appear that it is further constrained in meeting domestic needs.

Being aware that this is the case, it seems logical that Government moves to reduce unproductive spending. The fact that a social development policy is linked to Government's macroeconomics policy; and considering that built into the macroeconomics policy is government's reliance on foreign borrowing and funding from international donor agencies: and recognizing that many of these funding agencies are withdrawing or reducing levels of assistance, and moreover that fact that Barbados no longer qualifies for donor assistance based on its high ratings as a developing country, it is imperative that Government exercises stringency, in order to enable it to deliver on its social programmes.

Changing economic and social factors necessitate that the social development policy concerns itself with the small size of Barbados, its limited natural resources, the fragile tourism industry and the aging population. This brings me to reemphasize the point that Government has to develop innovative ways of employment creation, if it is to remove any added pressure on the social system. Added to this, it would require that new strategies be identified for securing funding to support programme initiatives. Out of necessity, no effort is to be spared to reduce the incidence of unemployment amongst the able bodied and employable citizens of this society. This means that people with disabilities ought to be fully integrated into the world of work.

Returning to the subject of providing quality and sustained employment, it is important that the social policy reflects a commitment to upholding the ILO's core labour standards, which speak principally to the right to decent work. It therefore means that a new vision should embrace the need to protect the fundamental rights of workers against employers who seek an unfair advantage, by way of the violation of the core labour standards.

Added to this, it becomes imperative that as part of the decent work agenda, that there is a recognition of the need to maintain a comprehensive social protection programme.In establishing a platform for sustainable growth, it demands that Government places continual emphasis on health care. These in essence are fundamental towards promoting longevity and a healthy population, and more so, sustain the work life of people, now that the age of retirement has moved to age sixty-five.

It is critical to this process that the policy of free health care remains, thus ensuring that the poor are not denied access to care. What remains a crucial matter is that Government addresses the question of migrant labour and its potential impact on its delivery of public services. Whilst it is important to look at the impact that migrant labour could have on housing and health care, the principal concern would be that of the retention of jobs by nationals. It is clear that

Government will have to shoulder greater responsibilities, if there is rampant unemployment amongst citizens.

We can conclude that a strong social policy is said to be essential for sustainable growth. The challenge to Barbados as far as social policy development is concerned, is to look to move beyond the realm of a state of social welfarism. This would be consistent with the thinking that is expressed in the Draft National Strategic Plan (2005-2025), that the move to eradicate poverty would be to remove the pressure placed on the island's limited resources.

In closing, I must reemphasize the need for wealth creation. Protocol V envisages wealth creation as a development strategy, since it carries with it sustainability which will guarantee social development. The first order of business should remain that of identifying what is needed for wealth creation, to be followed by a determination of how to implement what has been discovered through the establishment of a social partnership in Barbados."

Presentation on the topic delivered by Dennis de Peiza, General Secretary, Congress of Trade Unions and Staff Associations of Barbados ,September 27, 2005

The Employee Work Ethic

The issue of the work ethic of employees is emerging as a topical issue in many geographical jurisdictions. The interest in the subject is linked directly to what some employers claim to be declining workplace productivity, which may tend to impact negatively on the growth of the national economy.

Many theories have been advanced regarding the factors that contribute to a declining work ethic. The views shared may be influenced by one's interest; depending upon whether the perspective is aligned with employers or employees. Albeit, it can reasonably be argued that both employer and employee must share equal responsibility for any decline in the work ethic, whereever it exists.

What therefore is the basis of this assertion? To understand the premise of the argument, one ought to first understand what is meant by 'Work ethic.' The work ethic is usually associated with people who work hard and do a good job. The interpersonal skills of the employee that include attitudes, habits, manners, appearance, behaviour, along with exercise of initiative, being dependable and creative, are all reflective of a good work ethic.

Following on these attributes, the work ethic of an employee is driven by an employer who provides appropriate opportunities to make the job challenging. This serves as a stimulus to the employee, who is not only motivated, but is given the impetus to be creative. The long and short is that if a high work ethic is to be achieved and maintained, then it becomes the responsibility of managers and employers to find appropriate ways to make the job more fulfilling for employees.

Added to this, careful attention ought to be paid by employers to their human relations skills, if they are to diminish, or better yet, eliminate the existence of an adversarial relationship between employer and employees.

One sure way of achieving this would be for employers to desist from practising the authoritarian style of management. This style of management has no place in the contemporary world of work, where the emphasis has now been shifted to the participatory approach of management. It is felt that in today's workplace, management must have open communication with employees. This is essential to the building of the organization, as it gives rise to a shared vision for the organization, to the effort of realizing a common goal, and to cause the employees to feel a sense of ownership.

Employers can further contribute to enhancing the work ethic of employees if they seek to observe the fundamental rights of workers at work, and provide decent work, that includes the payment of a decent wage, and providing a safe and healthy work environment for employees. How can these be achieved? Employers must observe and respect the local labour laws and ILO Conventions and Recommendations to which the state is a signatoree

Workers must be allowed freedom of association, the right to join a trade union of choice and to bargain collectively. There should be no road block to the recognition of a trade union by a business entity. Employees should be provided with safe work, be able to work in a safe and healthy environment, be paid a decent wage for work done, work in an environment where there is no exploitation and harassment, where equity prevails, and where discrimination in any form does not exists. Equally important, they must be guaranteed security of tenure.

To further enhance the work ethic of employees, employers would do well to bolster employee confidence, build morale, create employee loyalty and satisfaction, motivate and stimulate greater levels of productivity, if every effort is made to properly recognize and reward the efforts of employees. Employers must come to grips with the fact that employees are their most valued resource. There must be recognition that if they are treated well, employees will be dependable, reliable, committed and dedicated to the job.

Employers must work at embracing their employees by valuing their contributions, efforts and ideas; developing mutual trust, being ethical in their actions, establishing a policy of open communication, and in the sharing of rewards.

It stands to reason that once the conditions are right, employees would exhibit a healthy work ethic. Be that as it may, it is important that employees demonstrate their commitment to playing their part by exhibiting a healthy work ethic. To start, they must exhibit an excellent character, one which reflects honesty, loyalty, discipline, trustworthiness, responsibility, being reliable, and willing to show initiative. Other qualities to be exhibited should include respect in dealing with people, co-operation with workplace colleagues inclusive of management personnel, leadership traits, being productive, demonstrating a positive attitude, being good team player, displaying organizational skills, such as time management. It is important that individual attention is paid to dress, etiquette and personal hygiene.

Wherever the subject of the work ethic of employees is debated, it is important that the debate is placed into context. If the factors outlined in this article are to mean anything, then it is important that any perceived decline in the work ethic cannot be premised on a stand alone action by either the employer or employee. The reality is that for a good work ethic to be achieved amongst employees, then there is seemingly a responsibility on the part of the employer to set the stage to make this happen. Where the employer fails and breaks the bond of good will, it is inevitable that this will lead to a breach in the relationship, with his/her employees who are no longer motivated.

How can the declining work ethic be arrested? To start with there ought to be recognition that today's work force strives on being rewarded. Where an employer fails to identify and meet with the standards and expectation of the work environment, then it can reasonably expected that workers will respond negatively. Where a poor work ethic exists within a work environment, it becomes the responsibility of the employer to work towards ensuring that the business entity sets and/or maintains standards in its operations towards developing a more motivated and committed group of employees. This goal is achievable if the employer works with the trade union, as the representative of labour, in establishing appropriate terms anc conditions of service for employess.

'The Unionist', Barbados Workers Union, Vol.11 No.5 2006

ABBREVIATIONS

ATM - Automatic Teller Machine

BARNAPCO - Barbados National Productivity Council

BEC - Barbados Employers Confederation

BSTU - Barbados Secondary Teachers Union

BUT - Barbados Union of Teachers

BWU - Barbados Workers Union

CNN - Canadian News Network

CSME - Caricom Single Market and Economy

CTUSAB - Congress of Trade Unions and Staff Associations of Barbados

CXC - Caribbean Examinations Council

DFID - Department for International Development

DLP - Democratic Labour Party

EDUTECH - Education Technical Enhancement Programme

ILO - International Labour Organization

NCPAD - National Council on the Prevention of Alcohol Dependency

NCSA - National Council of Substance Abuse

NUPW - National Union of Public Workers

PROMALCO - Promotion of Management Labour Cooperation

QEH - Queen Elizabeth Hospital

TUTTA - Trinidad & Tobago Unified Teachers Association

UWI - University of the West Indies.

www.ingramcontent.com/pod-product-compliance
Lightning Source LLC
Chambersburg PA
CBHW051641170526
45167CB00001B/285